Stenhouse Publishers
www.stenhouse.com

Copyright © 2014 by Janet Allen

All rights reserved. Except for the pages in the appendix, which may be photocopied for classroom use, no part of this publication may be reproduced or transmitted in any form or by any means, electronic or mechanical, including photocopy, or any information storage and retrieval system, without permission from the publisher.

Every effort has been made to contact copyright holders and students for permission to reproduce borrowed material. We regret any oversights that may have occurred and will be pleased to rectify them in subsequent reprints of the work.

Library of Congress Cataloging-in-Publication Data

Allen, Janet, 1950-
  Tools for teaching academic vocabulary / Janet Allen.
    pages cm
  ISBN 978-1-57110-408-3 (pbk. : alk. paper) 1. Vocabulary--Study and teaching. 2. Language arts. I. Title.
  LB1574.5.A44 2014
  372.44--dc23

                                      2014024902

Cover design, interior design, and typesetting by Martha Drury
Manufactured in the United States of America

20 19 18 17 16 15 14   9 8 7 6 5 4 3 2 1

DEDICATION

For Glenn—with love and gratitude for the constant encouragement (a.k.a. nagging). I'm sorry I didn't get this finished in time for Stenhouse to give you your easy chair in the exhibit hall booth!

ACKNOWLEDGMENTS

Professional writing is never easy, but the amazing people at Stenhouse certainly make the entire process seem smooth. Special thanks to Philippa Stratton—an editor whose patience is even longer than Job's and a friend whose support lasts even through the rough patches.

Many thanks to the students and teachers who generously shared their work with me. The pages of this text are enriched by your contributions.

Introduction

(• indicates a reproducible form in the appendix.)

Introduction

I don't think my handwriting has improved because I have been doing it "half fast."

—Fourth grader's self-assessment

If I were assessing my teaching of vocabulary, I would have to admit that my assessment would be similar to this fourth grader's self-assessment of his progress. Knowing no other options, I tried to teach and assess knowledge of words in the same ways I had been taught. Our district used programmed-vocabulary books and it seemed an "efficient" way to teach vocabulary. The troubling aspect for me was that students seldom used the words in their writing or speaking. I felt what I was doing wasn't really increasing their vocabulary, but I didn't know what else to do. I fell into the trap of seeing vocabulary as *something* we did but not part of *everything* we did.

The purpose of this text is to develop a deeper understanding for effective academic vocabulary instruction and provide you with tools to help your students learn new words, become more conscious of words, and increase competence in knowing when and how to use the words. Like the two previous flipcharts I've written—*Tools for Teaching Content Literacy* and *More Tools for Teaching Content Literacy*—*Tools for Teaching Academic Vocabulary* is not designed to provide you with a program. It is designed to provide you with resources to create your own program that meets the needs of your students and your learning goals, as well as the demands of rigorous texts and high-stakes assessments.

Tools for Teaching Academic Vocabulary begins with Developing a Comprehensive Vocabulary Program, which is an overview of the components of a research-based vocabulary program (Graves 2000, 2006). This is followed by Defining Types of Vocabulary: General Academic; Domain- or Discipline-Specific; Topic-Specific; and Passage-Critical (Text-Specific), with a quick reference chart (Reference Chart for Vocabulary Types) that highlights the salient characteristics for each type of vocabulary.

Following these introductory materials, you will find the instructional tools I have included to support teaching academic vocabulary. For ease of use, the tools are ordered based on the four components of effective vocabulary instruction. An overview page is provided for each of the four components followed by tools that can be used to develop effective instruction for that component.

As educators, we know it will take a wide variety of resources to ensure that all students experience the power of knowing and choosing the right word for any task. It is my hope that this resource will add to your existing repertoire for accomplishing that goal.

References

Allen, J. 2004. *Tools for Teaching Content Literacy*. Portland, ME: Stenhouse.

———. 2008. *More Tools for Teaching Content Literacy*. Portland, ME: Stenhouse.

Graves, M. F. 2000. "A Vocabulary Program to Complement and Bolster a Middle-Grade Comprehension Program." In *Reading for Meaning: Fostering Comprehension in the Middle Grades*, ed. B. M. Taylor, M. F. Graves, and P. van den Broek. Newark, DE: International Reading Association.

———. 2006. *The Vocabulary Book: Learning & Instruction*. New York: Teachers College Press.

Developing a Comprehensive Vocabulary Program

It is certainly possible to know the what of a thing without knowing the how or when of it.
— P. A. Alexander, D. L. Schallert, and V. C. Hare, "Coming to Terms"

With each new wave of literacy reform, we seem to know more of the "what" of vocabulary instruction without clearly knowing the "how" or "when" of that instruction. The publication and widespread adoption of the Common Core State Standards (2010) have heightened the discussion about the importance of effective teaching of vocabulary. However, all state standards include standards focused on increased knowledge of language. In spite of the pressure to meet and exceed standards, many educators say that creating a comprehensive vocabulary program that is effective, efficient, and engaging still eludes them.

Fortunately, today we have access to a great deal of research that documents and describes components of a comprehensive vocabulary program. Understanding these components and knowing how to focus instruction so all components support word learning in every classroom is critical. The components are not grade-level or discipline specific and should apply to any words you want students to learn. You may want to use the organizer on page A1 in the appendix (Graves 2006) to guide discussion and assess the degree to which these components are established and used in your classrooms.

1. **Providing Rich and Varied Language Experiences:** This component is a cornerstone for all instruction. If students have access, including time, to read, discuss, and write a wide variety of texts, they will encounter many unfamiliar words. The chart below shows the potential benefits (Nagy and Herman 1987).

Amount of Reading	Number of Days Reading	Number of Words Encountered	Number of Unfamiliar Words Encountered	Annual Gain in Vocabulary
25 minutes/day	200	1,000,000	15,000–30,000	700–1,500 words

2. **Teaching Individual Words:** Teaching individual words that are essential to content is critical, but the sheer volume of words that would need to be taught is overwhelming. Stahl and Fairbanks summarized the problem: "Since a vocabulary teaching program typically teaches 10 to 12 words a week or about 400 a year, of which perhaps 75% or 300 are learned, vocabulary instruction is not adequate to cope with the volume of new words that children need to learn and do learn without instruction" (1986, 100).

3. **Teaching Word-Learning Strategies:** This component is based on the importance of supporting students in becoming independent word learners. Vygotsky's words, "What a child can do in cooperation today, he can do alone tomorrow" (1962, 104), aptly describe the necessity of students knowing and using a wide range of strategies for learning words independently.

4. **Fostering Word Consciousness:** Word-consciousness activities are often the most engaging part of word study. Many activities fall into this component: activities involving word play, researching and sharing word origins, and helping students become aware of the structure, subtleties, and use of language.

References

Alexander, P. A., D. L. Schallert, and V. C. Hare. 1991. "Coming to Terms: How Researchers in Learning and Literacy Talk About Knowledge." *Review of Educational Research* 61 (3): 315–343.

Graves, M. F. 2006. *The Vocabulary Book: Learning & Instruction.* New York: Teachers College Press.

Nagy, W. E., and P. A. Herman. 1987. "Breadth and Depth of Vocabulary Knowledge: Implications for Acquisition and Instruction." In *The Nature of Vocabulary Acquisition*, ed. M. G. McKeown and M. E. Curtis. Hillsdale, NJ: Erlbaum.

National Governors Association (NGA) Center for Best Practices, Council of Chief State School Officers (CCSSO). 2010. Common Core State Standards. Washington, DC: NGA/CCSSO.

Stahl, S. A., and M. M. Fairbanks. 1986. "The Effects of Vocabulary Instruction: A Model-Based Meta-Analysis." *Review of Educational Research* 56 (1): 72–110.

Vygotsky, L. 1962. *Thought and Language.* Cambridge, MA: MIT Press.

Defining Types of Vocabulary

I'm not sure I know what that term means, but I think I'm already doing it.

—Virginia middle school teacher

The practice of replacing old words with new ones that may, or may not, be more precise can lead to confusion for educators. A common question I hear is: "Everyone is talking about teaching academic vocabulary, but how is that different from what I'm already doing?" A brief response to this question is that academic vocabulary is the language that is used to comprehend and communicate within or across academic disciplines or content areas. However, under the umbrella of this definition, there are types of academic vocabulary, and all types of academic vocabulary would not be taught using the same methods.

In an attempt not to add to the confusion about terms, I want to describe the four types of academic vocabulary I address in *Tools for Teaching Academic Vocabulary*. While these terms are used with increasing frequency, not everyone would categorize or use these types of words in the same way. In order to provide a common language for my writing and your reading, I have defined and described the terms as I use them. These definitions and descriptions should help you determine the type and frequency of vocabulary on which you will focus based on your teaching and learning goals.

General Academic Vocabulary

These are words used across disciplines rather than words that are specific to a single discipline or domain. These words are used in the CCSS, in other state standards or learning results, and in the questions and prompts students encounter on standardized tests. Students will encounter these words in any discipline. They are often verbs as they usually indicate the cognitive processes or actions students must employ to complete a task. Based on their frequency of use, I would classify these as Tier 2 words (Beck, McKeown, and Kucan 2002).

Domain- or Discipline-Specific Vocabulary

These words are a constant in a given discipline. I view these words as a subset of academic vocabulary as they are critical to understanding the discipline and the tasks associated with that discipline. In the context of a specific content area, these words would be considered Tier 2 words, as they are high-utility words in that discipline. They may be encountered in other contexts, but they are most often and definitely necessary to comprehend, use, and communicate the content of a given domain or discipline. In general usage, these terms might be considered Tier 3 words if encountered infrequently.

Topic-Specific Vocabulary

Topic-specific words are a subset of discipline- or domain-specific words. These words are related to a unit or topic of study that occurs within a discipline. Usually, these words are Tier 3 words because they are related to a specific domain and may have a lower frequency of use than the discipline-specific words since they are connected to a single topic within that discipline.

Passage-Critical (Text-Specific) Vocabulary

Passage-critical words are words students don't know, are critical to understanding a specific text passage, and can't be defined from their repertoire of word-learning strategies. Categorizing these words as any one tier would be difficult; they might be rare (Tier 3) but critical to comprehension, or they might be basic words (Tier 1) that readers still don't know. Therefore, these are words I would target for direct instruction.

References

Beck, I. L., M. G. McKeown, and L. Kucan. 2002. *Bringing Words to Life: Robust Vocabulary Instruction*. New York: Guilford.

Reference Chart for Vocabulary Types

Word Types with Examples	Critical Features	Tier	Instructional Implications
General Academic Examples: *analyze, cite, compare, determine, develop, recount, restate, summarize*	• Not discipline-specific so encountered frequently • Usually indicate task or action being required • Necessary for understanding prompts, questions, or directives	Tier 2	Since these words are widely used, in-depth instruction and frequent use is required so cognitive action is automatic. The words should be used in classroom activities, in-depth discussions, learning tasks, and preparation for testing.
Domain- or Discipline-Specific Math: *fraction, integer, ratio* English: *conflict, genre, plot* Science: *formulate, hypothesis, observation* Music: *dynamic markings, lyrics, measure, tempo*	• Discipline-specific • Frequently used and repeated as the language of the discipline • Language necessary for reading, writing, listening, and speaking about the content	Tier 3	These words would be cumulative in a discipline so frequent references to the words and their use would be critical.
Topic-Specific Photosynthesis: *chlorophyll, endothermic, exothermic, photoautotrophs* Holocaust: *extermination, Nazis, persecuted, systematic, regime*	• Topic-specific • Necessary to understand and communicate learning about the topic	Tier 3	These words are critical to comprehension and communication of information about a topic or concept so direct instruction and guided practice about how the words connect to the topic or concept would be necessary.
Passage-Critical In *BATS: Biggest! Littlest!* (Markle 2013): *echolocation, homing, roost, wingspan* In *ICE! The Amazing History of the Ice Business* (Pringle 2012): *chisel, sawdust, thaw*	• Context-specific • Words critical for understanding a specific passage or entire text	Usually Tier 1 or 3	These words are critical to understanding passage of text so direct instruction would be required if the word is common or basic. If the word is rare, you might want to give students the definition within the context and help them see how and why the word was used.

References

Markle, S. 2013. *BATS: Biggest! Littlest!* Honesdale, PA: Boyds Mills Press.
Pringle, L. 2012. *ICE! The Amazing History of the Ice Business.* Honesdale, PA: Calkins Creek.

Providing Rich and Varied Language Experiences

My language is changing. I don't understand it. I read all those books and then I find these words just coming out of my mouth. I don't even know where they come from.

—Sarah, grade ten

What Does It Mean to Provide Rich and Varied Language Experiences?

Sarah's announcement is a living example of Stahl's research: "The amount of reading that people do is directly related to their knowledge of word meanings, even after accounting for intelligence. One obvious way then to increase the number of words children know is to increase the amount of text to which they are exposed" (1999, 13). We could look to many researchers and find agreement in terms that rich and varied language experiences are the foundation for all vocabulary instruction. And most would agree that those rich experiences begin with increasing the volume and diversity of reading in which students participate. Those experiences can range from your reading aloud to students to their participation in shared, guided, and independent reading.

However, rich and varied experiences should include more than reading. James Britton says that "writing floats on a sea of talk" (1970, 64). In trying to establish a *productive* "sea of talk" in a classroom, you will want to create opportunities for students to read and write and to discuss their reading and writing with others, but you will also want to provide them with time to develop expressive ways to communicate in print and nonprint media. Many language experiences can directly support students in learning language without taking a great deal of time. These activities can support comprehension and increase students' verbal and writing fluency in your discipline.

How Do Varied Language Experiences Support Learning?

Providing time in school and support out of school for students to increase the volume and diversity of reading is absolutely essential in terms of learning new words. With the large amount of content students encounter in each discipline, it is necessary that they develop a working knowledge of the language of each discipline. Moore, Readence, and Rickelman cite the importance of being able to recognize and use disciplinary language:

"Outsiders are restricted in their communication with a group because they cannot use the group's special vocabulary and the concepts inherent in that terminology. Insiders use special vocabulary freely to communicate with the collective members of a group" (1989, 36). Some of the development of this disciplinary "insider" language can occur through a variety of rich language experiences prior to and during immersion in the content. Common prereading activities such as word sorts, possible sentences, or information passes can provide students with engaging opportunities to encounter and discuss the disciplinary language necessary to help them comprehend and communicate in your class.

References

Britton, J. 1970. *Language and Learning*. Harmondsworth, Middlesex, GB: Penguin.

Moore, D. W., J. E. Readence, and R. J. Rickelman. 1989. *Prereading Activities for Content Area Reading and Learning*. 2nd ed. Newark, DE: International Reading Association.

Stahl, S. A. 1999. *Vocabulary Development: From Reading Research to Practice*. Newton Upper Falls, MA: Brookline Books.

Read, Reflect, Respond, & Remember

I could open a book, and I could be anything. I could be anywhere. I could be anyone. My friends, I read myself out of poverty long before I worked myself out of poverty.
—Walter Anderson

What Is Read, Reflect, Respond, & Remember?

When I asked my ninth-grade students, "What gets in the way of reading for you?" they were brutally honest in their responses. "Too much time doing other stuff. There's never enough time to *really* read." Most researchers would agree with my students. Many studies are highlighted throughout this text where the findings include the importance of providing rich and varied language experiences as a component for increasing vocabulary. Volume and diversity of reading is the foundation on which other aspects of vocabulary instruction stand. In classrooms across the country, teachers use a variety of methods for students to track those reading experiences: journals, academic reading logs, projects, and discussion. Read, Reflect, Respond, & Remember is a graphic organizer that gives students an opportunity to track their reading, reflect on their learning, and focus on one or more new words they want to remember from that reading. A blank version is included on page A2 of the appendix.

How Could Read, Reflect, Respond, & Remember Work in the Classroom?

There are many ways to provide rich reading experiences, and this organizer provides students with an opportunity to think about their independent reading in terms of content *and* new or unknown words.

1. Provide students with a large selection of books from which they can choose independent reading books. These collections should include fiction and nonfiction. If you want students to read books that support learning in your discipline, provide them with a library of discipline-specific titles. For example, in math, Campbell's *Mysterious Patterns* (2014) might be one of the choices for independent reading.
2. Set aside time for in-class reading or ask students to read the book outside of class.
3. Ask students to respond to some or all of the prompts on Read, Reflect, Respond, & Remember. While it isn't necessary to respond to all of the prompts, it is necessary

that they complete what they want to remember and how the chosen word of the day connects to what they learned. The example on page A3 in the appendix is a sample based on *Mysterious Patterns*.
4. Occasionally, you might want to ask students to share the books they read and the words they learned with group members. This will facilitate students being introduced to books they might not have previously considered. Also, you may want to note their misinterpretations, inadequate definitions, or misunderstandings as content for future instruction.

When and Why Should I Use Read, Reflect, Respond, & Remember?

Students could complete this organizer every day they do independent reading, at the end of the week as a summary of that week's reading, or when they finish a book. Use of any graphic organizer should be frequent enough so the organizer is a familiar way for them to connect abstract concepts to concrete learning. At a time when students are bombarded with information and technical or specialized language, it has become even more critical for students to encounter rich language in a variety of engaging texts. Research focused on increasing word knowledge stresses the importance of providing students with rich reading experiences in addition to direct instruction. Blachowicz and Fisher remind us that "the strength of a program that allows students to select their own books is that they are more likely to read and to become involved in their reading" (2006, 85). Some of the words students learn through these reading experiences will be internalized solely from the context; however, other new or specialized words will need students to make a conscious effort to remember the words by using writing and graphics to document their learning.

References

Anderson, W. 1994. Personal communication. International Reading Association Third North American Conference on Adult and Adolescent Literacy. Washington, DC.

Blachowicz, C., and P. J. Fisher. 2006. *Teaching Vocabulary in All Classrooms.* 3rd ed. Upper Saddle River, NJ: Pearson Education.

Campbell, Sarah C. 2014. *Mysterious Patterns: Finding Fractals in Nature.* Honesdale, PA: Boyds Mills.

Word Talk with Word Questioning

I tried to put my mind back on Paradise Lost, *but it was hard going. Somniferous was my word of the day. It means sleep inducing, and it was a good one to describe that dull and endless poem. Milton meant to give us a glimpse of hell, Miss Wilcox said, and he succeeded.*
—Jennifer Donnelly, *A Northern Light*

What Is Word Talk?

Word talk is the active discussion, clarification, refinement, and questioning that occurs in situations that are designed for students to encounter and discuss content-related vocabulary. The lesson you design might provide a structured opportunity for students to encounter, discuss, and debate domain- or topic-specific vocabulary prior to encountering those words in the texts they will read. This discussion is a rich source for you in assessing the depth and breadth of content knowledge students bring to the unit of study. As students encounter the words they have previously talked about, they are able to contextualize their earlier discussion which leads to deeper understanding.

How Could Word Talk Work in the Classroom?

Increasing the word talk in your classroom could range from relatively incidental learning to structured activities. Word talk could occur before beginning the study of a topic in order to assess and build prior knowledge of the topic-specific words, and it could occur after the reading to solidify students' understanding of key information related to the topic.

When and Why Should I Use Word Talk?

In the context of providing students with a total language experience, Johnson and Pearson highlight the importance of talk in learning new words: "The best way we have found to reach our goal is to insist that by the end of any lesson a total language experience has been offered. That is, any vocabulary lesson must encourage students to really experience new words—to hear them used, to discuss and define meanings, to read or write them in meaningful context" (1984, 19–20). One of the greatest challenges for students is understanding content-specific vocabulary. If these words are only encountered in the text without any prior opportunity for students to see and talk about those words, there is a good chance they will understand only a small portion of what they read. Ideally, word talk should be used when students encounter a new word or categories of words related to content they will be reading.

Word Knowledge Through Questioning

Provide student groups with a list of domain- or topic-specific words from the new topic or unit of study. Ask students to discuss them based on their knowledge of the words and the topic and respond to the questions you provide. The following word-questioning activity is based on the topic of malnutrition.

- How are <u>vitamin B</u>, <u>milled rice</u>, and <u>beriberi</u> related?
- What possible connection could there be between <u>pirates</u> and <u>vitamin C</u>?
- What is the relationship between <u>growth spurts</u> and <u>empty-calorie foods</u>? (Choose two words that would seem to be unrelated.)
- How are <u>scurvy</u>, <u>diets</u>, and <u>picky eaters</u> all related to <u>malnutrition</u>?
- If I discovered <u>a cure for malnutrition</u>, what scientific words would likely describe the process I used?

The figure provides an additional example, which students will discuss prior to reading Jurmain's *The Secret of the Yellow Death: A True Story of Medical Sleuthing* (2009). The questions will be revisited and revised throughout the reading of this informational text. A blank version is included on page A4 of the appendix.

Word Talk with Word Questioning

Directions: Demonstrate your knowledge of the underlined words by using those words to respond to each of the questions.

1. How are <u>autopsies</u>, <u>microscopes</u>, and <u>test tubes</u> related in *The Secret of the Yellow Death*?
2. What possible connection could there be between <u>bouillon</u> and <u>yellow fever</u>?
3. What is the relationship between <u>mosquitoes</u> and *Bacillus icteroides*?
4. How are <u>Cuba</u>, <u>the battleship Maine</u>, <u>the Spanish-American War</u>, and <u>Dr. Walter Reed</u> all related to <u>yellow fever</u>?
5. If I noted the use of gelatin, bouillon, and bacillus, <u>where would I probably be</u>? <u>Why would I be using these words</u>?

References

Donnelly, Jennifer. 2003. *A Northern Light*. New York: Harcourt.

Johnson, D. D., and P. D. Pearson. 1984. *Teaching Reading Vocabulary*. 2nd ed. New York: Holt, Rinehart and Winston.

Jurmain, S. 2009. *The Secret of the Yellow Death: A True Story of Medical Sleuthing*. New York: Houghton Mifflin Harcourt.

Words from the Inside Out

Our knowledge of words determines how we understand texts, define ourselves for others, and define the way we see the world. A richer vocabulary does not just mean that we know more words, but that we have more complex and exact ways of talking about the world, and of understanding the ways that more complex thinkers see the world.

—Steven A. Stahl, *Vocabulary Development*

What Is Words from the Inside Out?

One part of providing students with opportunities for rich and varied language experiences is providing time and structure for students to immerse themselves in words. Words from the Inside Out is a graphic organizer that guides students in independently generating topic-specific words; collaboratively discussing, combining, and categorizing their words; and using their words to anticipate the content of a topic they are about to study. A blank version can be found on page A5 of the appendix. The initial activity is based on Taba's List-Group Label (1967) and is extended to provide focused talk to anticipate upcoming content. Jacobs states that "we understand the words we actually use. If students do not use these words, then they will not understand them, especially in high-stress testing situations (2006, 28). This activity will provide students with an opportunity to generate and discuss words, but it will also give them the opportunity to predict and use their words.

How Could Words from the Inside Out Work in the Classroom?

As the name of the organizer implies, the goal of this activity is to get students' prior knowledge of topic-related words from the inside out so they can be discussed. The following basic steps can be modified to fit your instructional goals:

1. Introduce students to the upcoming text or topic with a short text or visual. For example, if beginning to study scorpions in science, you might share the Roald Dahl poem from *Dirty Beasts* (1983) or simply give students time to examine the cover of *SCORPIONS! Strange and Wonderful* by Pringle (2013).
2. Ask each student to use the A–Z boxes and list all the words they think of when they think of scorpions. See the figure, based on students' beginning lists of words. Allow students to list as many words as they want, but you will probably want to give them a minimum number of words.
3. After each student generates a word list, ask students to work in small groups to combine all their words in a group A–Z chart.

4. After words are combined, students should use the space at the bottom of the organizer to categorize and label their words. For example, they may come up with categories such as characteristics of scorpions, dangers of being around scorpions, habits and habitats of scorpions.
5. Following this activity, ask students to predict what they think they will learn or how they think some of their words might be used in the upcoming study of scorpions.
6. During the reading and study that follow this activity, students can collect other scorpion-related words and add them to their A–Z chart for use when they do academic writing about this topic.

Words from the Inside Out: Scorpions			
A–B	C–D constellation, deserts	E–F fast	G–H
I–J	K–L	M–N	O–P poisonous, predators
Q–R	S–T scary, sting, stinger, tail, Texas	U–V venom	WXYZ
Characteristics of scorpions	Dangers of being around scorpions	Habits and habitats of scorpions	

When and Why Should I Use Words from the Inside Out?

While this activity can be used at any time, it is most helpful when it is part of the study of a new text or topic. It allows you to assess some of the prior knowledge students have about the topic. In addition, it allows students to collaborate and learn some of the topic-specific language that all students have shared. Finally, it gives students an opportunity to think about the topic and anticipate how those words might be used in the reading they will do. These predictions can be revisited and revised based on new information students gain from the related texts they read.

References

Dahl, R. 1983. *Dirty Beasts*. New York: Penguin. http://www.youtube.com/watch?v=5ORdpSbpbpM

Jacobs, H. H. 2006. *Active Literacy Across the Curriculum: Strategies for Reading, Writing, Speaking and Listening*. Larchmont, NY: Eye on Education.

Pringle, L. 2013. *SCORPIONS! Strange and Wonderful*. Honesdale, PA: Boyds Mills.

Stahl, S. A. 1999. *Vocabulary Development: From Reading Research to Practice*. Newton Upper Falls, MA: Brookline Books.

Taba, H. 1967. *Teacher's Handbook for Elementary Social Studies*. Reading, MA: Addison-Wesley.

Teaching Individual Words

Teaching specific terms in a specific way is probably the strongest action a teacher can take to ensure that students have the academic background knowledge they need to understand the content they will encounter in school.
—Marzano and Pickering, *Building Academic Vocabulary*

The "How Should I Teach Vocabulary?" Dilemma

When asked about their methods for teaching vocabulary, many teachers immediately think of teaching individual words. The common practice of assigning lists of words and asking students to find definitions and create sentences has long been the essence of vocabulary instruction in many classrooms. As a student, it was how I was "taught" vocabulary, and as a teacher it was how I "taught" vocabulary. It was years into my teaching career before I ever considered what it really meant to know a word. Like many other teachers, I knew my vocabulary instruction was ineffective, but I didn't know what to do if I eliminated the word lists, definitions, and sentences.

Fortunately, now we have both research and descriptions of classroom practices that highlight effective ways to teach individual words. Unfortunately, knowing which words to teach and how to teach those words is still a complex process. Part of the complexity of the task is related to what it really means to know a word and the purpose learners will have for knowing that word.

What Does It Mean to Know a Word?

Many researchers have tackled the question of what it means to know a word. If you can recognize it and pronounce it, does it mean you know the word? I think we could all agree with Nagy's assertion that "reading comprehension depends on a wealth of encyclopedic knowledge and not merely on definitional knowledge of the words in the text" (1988, 7). Understanding what it means to know a word is critical because it informs you about the depth of word knowledge your students will need in order to use the word. Knowing any word can range on a continuum from never having seen, heard, or experienced the word to being able to use the word in speech and writing and knowing when and where the word would be appropriate.

How Does This Information Impact Instruction?

Given that there is limited time for direct instruction of individual words, it is critical that we choose wisely which words to teach. Many teachers categorize words using Beck, McKeown,

and Kucan's (2002) three tiers, placing instructional emphasis for direct instruction on Tier 2 words. These are the words that are encountered frequently and have the greatest impact on verbal fluency. In deciding which words students would need to know, it is important to think about the purpose for the word knowledge. Is it a general academic word that is used across disciplines and will be frequently encountered or is it a word students need to know to understand a passage they are reading? The tools that follow can be used for in-depth instruction of the most critical vocabulary (general academic); instruction focused on categories of related words (domain- or topic-specific); and limited instruction for low-frequency, passage-critical words. The breadth of anticipated use will help you determine the depth of instruction.

References

Beck, I. L., M. G. McKeown, and L. Kucan. 2002. *Bringing Words to Life: Robust Vocabulary Instruction*. New York: Guilford.

Marzano, R. J., and D. J. Pickering. 2005. *Building Academic Vocabulary: Teacher's Manual*. Alexandria, VA: Association for Supervision and Curriculum Development.

Nagy, W. E. 1988. *Teaching Vocabulary to Improve Reading Comprehension*. Newark, DE: International Reading Association.

5 W's and H of Knowing a Word

"When I use a word," Humpty Dumpty said in rather a scornful tone, "it means just what I choose it to mean—neither more nor less."

"The question is," said Alice, "whether you can make words mean so many different things."

"The question is," said Humpty Dumpty, "which is to be master—that's all."

—Lewis Carroll, *Through the Looking Glass*

What Is 5 W's and H of Knowing a Word?

As educators, we have all seen oral and written examples of students using sentences that indicate their knowledge of a word is one-dimensional or even incorrect. While these sentences can be extremely humorous, it is easy to see how shallow knowledge of a word could have a significant impact on comprehension. In *Teaching Mathematics Vocabulary in Context*, Murray highlights the complexity of knowing a word: "Constructing word knowledge involves developing meaning over time through many rich encounters in a variety of contexts, and using a variety of strategies, ranging from incidental references to direct instruction" (2004, 23). The graphic organizer on page A6 in the appendix provides students with a series of considerations when learning new words. Each of the sentence-starter words in the first column is extended into a question about the target word. The completed one shown here contains the questions I used, but a blank one is provided on page A7 of the appendix so you can create question extensions that support learning vocabulary in your content area.

How Could the 5 W's and H of Knowing a Word Work in the Classroom?

Use the graphic organizer to guide your students through steps they can take to gain in-depth knowledge of a word.

1. Introduce students to the lesson by sharing some examples of misused words in order to illustrate the importance of knowing a word. If you don't have examples, there are many on websites such as http://examples.yourdictionary.com/examples/examples-of-malapropism.html.
2. Explain to students that with the widespread use of academic vocabulary across all disciplines, in conversations, and in testing situations, it is critical that they have deep knowledge of these words. Give them a few examples of general academic words and ask them to add others commonly used in their classes.
3. Use the organizer and guide students through one of the general academic or discipline-specific words used in a text or on an assessment. For a general academic word such as *interpret*, I would modify the questions as shown on page A8 in the appendix. When possible, choose a word that is naturally occurring in a text or task for the day.
4. Brainstorm other ways students could know a word. In Sprenger's book *Teaching the Critical Vocabulary of the Common Core* (2013), she provides several ways for students to know words: definition, synonyms, jingles that demonstrate knowledge of the word, movement activities, and examples. You may want to add these to the strategies students offer.
5. Give students time to add this general academic word to their word cards or academic notebooks.
6. Take the opportunity to revisit previous words as new words are taught. Occasionally, give students a chance to note examples of the word being used in other classes or contexts.

When and Why Should I Use Knowing a Word?

Whether you have created a schoolwide list of general academic words or created a list for your discipline, I would recommend you teach a new word every two or three days. This work is important for all students but it is critical for students in poverty. In Jensen's *Engaging Students with Poverty in Mind* (2013), he notes that low socioeconomic status puts children at risk for academic failure. This makes the teacher's role even more critical in their lives. Jensen says: "Academic vocabulary—the vocabulary students need in order to understand the concepts and content taught in the various subject areas and to succeed on tests—is particularly critical. Teachers must be relentless about using nonverbal communication, visual aids, and context to add meaning and incorporate vocabulary building with engagement activities whenever appropriate" (2013, 12). The importance of this became clear to me when working in state assessment testing. I realized that if students know the content but not what they are being asked to do, they will struggle in school—and in standardized testing.

References

Carroll, L. 1946. *Through the Looking Glass*. New York: Grosset and Dunlap.

Jensen, E. 2013. *Engaging Students with Poverty in Mind: Practical Strategies for Raising Achievement*. Alexandria, VA: Association for Supervision and Curriculum Development.

Murray, M. 2004. *Teaching Mathematics Vocabulary in Context: Windows, Doors, and Secret Passageways*. Portsmouth, NH: Heinemann.

Sprenger, M. 2013. *Teaching the Critical Vocabulary of the Common Core: 55 Words That Make or Break Student Understanding*. Alexandria, VA: Association for Supervision and Curriculum Development.

Comparison by Analysis

If words are stored in categories, then it makes sense to teach them that way.

—Steven A. Stahl, *Vocabulary Development*

What Is Comparison by Analysis?

Comparison by analysis describes the practice of grouping words together for extended discussion and definition related to the differences between and among the words. Vocabulary instruction focused on general academic words needs a two-pronged approach where students are taught individual words and then they are guided in exploring the differences between similar academic terms. Comparison by Analysis is simply a graphic organizer to help students move beyond knowing a definition for a word and to examining closely what the characteristics are that make two or more similar words unique in terms of the cognitive task being required. I've included a blank version on page A9 of the appendix.

How Could Comparison by Analysis Work in the Classroom?

You may want to categorize similar general academic words into clusters that describe the actions one is being asked to perform when these words are used in prompts or other tasks. There are many resources where this has been done, and any one of those resources could help you create your own categories (Burke 2013; Marzano and Simms 2013; Sprenger 2013). Each of these texts not only identifies general academic terms but also provides a description of the cognitive action required. In the example shown in the figure, I combined *paraphrase, retell, summarize,* and *synthesize* as a cluster of related academic vocabulary words. Students work collaboratively to define each word and generate its characteristics. Then, in their own words, they explain what they are being asked to do when that term is used. Some of the clusters I use most often are shown in the following chart:

delineate	analyze	comprehend	articulate
determine	evaluate	explain	cite
identify	interpret	infer	describe
locate	trace	integrate	distinguish

These general academic terms are used frequently across disciplines, in the CCSS and other state standards, and on assessments. The most critical aspect of this instruction is not the memorization of words and definitions; it is the increased awareness and knowledge of the actions required by the terms. After several lessons, asking students to create pairs or clusters of words that still confuse them will be a critical piece of this instruction.

When and Why Should I Use Comparison by Analysis?

In many schools and classrooms, teachers have identified general academic vocabulary necessary for students to succeed in content

Comparison by Analysis

General Academic Vocabulary	Definition	Unique Characteristics	In my own words, this means I'm being asked to . . .
paraphrase	Restate the original text, giving the meaning in another form.	Usually as long, or longer, than the original text.	*Say the same things the author said but use my own words.*
retell	Tell a story again in your own way.	A retelling can be verbal or written. It can include inferences and opinions.	*Say or write the intent of the author's words. I can emphasize parts I consider important.*
summarize	Express in a form more concise than the original text.	Shorter than a paraphrase. Includes only important info. Doesn't include my opinions.	*Note the key ideas and significant details and combine into a condensed form.*
synthesize	Combine or blend all elements into a comprehensive, unified text.	Shorter than paraphrase. It is a conclusion of ideas and information.	*Take all the author's points or key ideas and combine in a logical conclusion based on text.*

classes and life. These non-discipline-specific words can name cognitive processes (e. g., *describe, identify, integrate*); features of text (*caption, cover, title*); structures of text (*cause/effect, sequence/chronology*); literary language (*character traits, conflict, plot*); and type of text (*documentary, political cartoon, script*). The most common focus for instruction across all disciplines is teaching students the names and actions required of the verbs that name cognitive processes. In Marzano and Simms's comprehensive approach detailed in *Vocabulary for the Common Core* (2013), the authors determined 227 verbs that identified cognitive processes used in the CCSS and divided those words into twenty-four basic categories. While each of the words should be taught with direct instruction in one or more classrooms, it is also important that students know the differences in what they are being asked to do when they see these words as part of a task. Knowing a definition—including unique characteristics of a general academic term—and taking it to a higher level of knowing how words differ in terms of task required is the kind of learning Comparison by Analysis supports. This kind of in-depth instruction is not easy or fast. I think most students would agree with Anderson's narrator in *Speak* when she is talking about her teacher: "Words are hard work. I hope they send Hairwoman to a conference or something. I'm ready to help pay for a sub" (2006, 85).

References

Anderson, L. H. 2006. *Speak*. New York: Penguin Books.

Burke, J. 2013. *The Common Core Companion: The Standards Decoded.* Thousand Oaks, CA: Corwin.

Marzano, R. J., and J. A. Simms. 2013. *Vocabulary for the Common Core.* Bloomington, IN: Marzano Research Laboratory.

Sprenger, M. 2013. *Teaching the Critical Vocabulary of the Common Core: 55 Words That Make or Break Student Understanding.* Alexandria, VA: Association for Supervision and Curriculum Development.

Stahl, S. A. 1999. *Vocabulary Development: From Reading Research to Practice.* Upper Newton Falls, MA: Brookline Books.

Word Logs

I think several things happen when students pick words for study. First, of course, the words are theirs, they feel ownership and, often, pride. They are also "experts" on their words and are willing to share their insights with the rest of the class.
—John A. Ianacone, "Vocabulary Lists"

What Are Word Logs?

When learning individual words or groups of words, it is important that students are involved in the process of committing the words to memory and use. Word logs are student-created records of new, interesting, important, or noteworthy words that can help meet those goals. Word logs can range from short-term collections of words that support learning-specific content to a daily log of new and interesting words. Dale and O'Rourke noted that "for many children the act of writing a word and its definition will help in remembering it later" (1986, 113). That is the purpose of any word log—collecting words in order to increase students' working vocabularies. Word logs can be as simple as noting words and definitions or extended to include contexts, examples, and visual notes. Word logs can be independent activities or whole-class activities where students' individual word choices are shared as part of a whole-class selection of important words students will explore and learn (Haggard 1982).

How Could Word Logs Work in the Classroom?

Word logs can and should take many forms in a classroom. The most important aspect is that whatever is used would add to a student's knowledge of words. As you can see from the following classroom examples, different types of logs are used depending on each teacher's preferences and instructional goals.

In science, students keep a cumulative record of the domain-specific words they are using. They place a three-hole-punched manila folder in their notebooks. Each of the four sides of the folder is divided into six squares where students write the domain-specific science words. A sheet of paper is inserted behind the manila folder so students can write definitions, examples, and graphics to support memory. The example on page A10 in the appendix is from a middle school science class.

In social studies, students use the organizer Collaborate for Understanding: Think-Pair-Share to develop an understanding of passage-critical words (see page A11 in the appendix for a blank version). Students individually attempt to define the word from a context and their background knowledge. They then work in pairs to reach a collaborative definition. Finally, they share their definition in a visual they have created as a cue for the word's meaning. Page A12 in the appendix shows an example based on the organizer.

In English Language Arts, students use a Portable Word Wall (see figure; a blank version can be found on page A13 of the appendix) as they read *Tuck Everlasting* (Babbitt 1974). The Portable Word Wall gives students the opportunity to note new or interesting words they want to save for use in their text-related writing. They write words on the organizer and use the reverse side of the paper to write brief notes to help them remember how each word was used.

All students keep individual Academic Vocabulary Cards—one large card with four individual sections on the front—as a way to keep track of academic vocabulary used across disciplines (see page A14 in the appendix for a guideline for creating these cards). The student sample shown on page A15 in the appendix helps a student remember the word *infer*. Students use a ring to keep the cards in their notebooks and add additional information on the reverse side of the index card when they encounter or use the word in any class.

When and Why Should I Use Word Logs?

There is no right or wrong way to use word logs, but it is important to create a consistent way for students to collect words, extend their understanding of the meanings of words, and use the words in appropriate contexts. Marzano and Simms note that "knowing what words mean and how they interconnect creates networks of knowledge that allow students to connect new information to previously learned information" (2013, 5). Word logs are the ideal way to help your students make connections between and among words they encounter.

Portable Word Wall for *Tuck Everlasting*

References

Babbitt, H. N. 1974. *Tuck Everlasting*. New York: Farrar, Straus and Giroux.

Dale, E., and J. O'Rourke. 1986. *Vocabulary Building: A Process Approach*. Columbus, OH: Zaner-Boser.

Haggard, M. R. 1982. "The Vocabulary Self-Selection Strategy: An Active Approach to Word Learning." *Journal of Reading* 26: 203–207.

Ianacone, J. A. 1993. "Vocabulary Lists: The Ambsace of Word Study." *English Journal* December: 41–45.

Marzano, R. J., and J. A. Simms. 2013. *Vocabulary for the Common Core*. Bloomington, IN: Marzano Research Laboratory.

Multiple-Meaning Words: From General to Domain-Specific Knowledge

One of the greatest sources of vocabulary development lies not so much in learning new words as in learning other meanings for words already known.
—E. Dale and J. O'Rourke, *Vocabulary Building*

What Are Multiple-Meaning Words?

Words with multiple meanings are referred to as polysemous words because they have two or more meanings. There are many details that can make a word have multiple meanings. In fact, if you look in a dictionary, you will discover that most words can have multiple meanings. The chart below highlights the most common types of multiple-meaning words. When you add other nuances such as contranyms (words that can mean the opposite, such as *clip*, which can mean to separate or to attach); capitalization (*will, Will*); parts of speech (*move*—noun or verb); and tense (*read, read*), it is easy to see why multiple-meaning words can make comprehension overwhelming.

Type	Spelling	Pronunciation	Meaning	Example
Homonyms	Same or Different	Same	Different	*Key* (used to unlock; low island reef)
Homophones (type of homonym)	Different	Same	Different	*To, too, two; bow, bough*
Homographs	Same	Same or Different	Different	*Lie* (untruth; *lie* down)
Heteronyms (type of homograph)	Same	Different	Different	*Tear* (trip or pull apart) *Tear* (fluid in/from the eye)

How Could Teaching Multiple-Meaning Words Work in the Classroom?

Teaching multiple-meaning words can be a daunting task because there are so many types. After introducing your students to different types of multiple-meaning words, I believe the most effective tool is teaching each word at the point of need. Whenever you encounter a domain-specific word students may know from another context, it is important to teach and talk about the word as it is used in the context of your discipline.

In the example shown in the figure, the teacher is using this organizer as a word wall to keep a cumulative record of the domain-specific math words students are learning. Students keep a copy of the organizer in their academic journals as well so they can keep track of each new math term that is is a known word from another context. Students brainstorm definitions or details related to what they already know about the word, note the math definition, and create a visual to help them remember the new definition. This organizer is one used in math class, but a generic form (Expert Language) is provided on page A16 in the appendix, as the same process can be used for helping students learn the language of any domain or discipline. For example, in PE some multiple-meaning words might be *court, foul,* or *score*. Regardless of the type of multiple-meaning words you are teaching, three critical components of effective instruction should still be employed: integration, repetition, and meaningful use (Stahl 1986).

When and Why Should I Teach Multiple-Meaning Words?

The most important reason for teaching students about multiple-meaning words is the impact on comprehension. Words that look the same but have different meanings can lead to ambiguity for any reader. However, these polysemous words can be particularly challenging for readers with limited language and a low volume of reading. The more limited students are in terms of depth of word knowledge, the more likely they are to struggle with reading and the more limited they will be in terms of word choice in writing and speaking. Many struggling readers simply give up when they experience confusion with a multiple-meaning word because that confusion can make all other surrounding sentences confusing.

In addition, many students assume that knowing a definition for a word means that they know the word. This thinking is reinforced each time we give students lists of words out of context and ask them to provide the definition for each word. However, knowing a definition for a word is the lowest level of word knowledge. Stahl notes that "a full and flexible knowledge of a word involves an understanding of the core meaning of a word and how it changes in different contexts" (1999, 25). Making students aware of the importance of context when encountering multiple-meaning words is critical so students begin to see patterns of multiple-meaning words they might encounter in your class.

Expert Language: Math			
Word	General meaning usage is . . .	In math it means . . .	Visual to help me remember . . .
base	bottom of something, support	number that is raised to a power in a mathematical expression	2^3
power	strength, the ability to do something	another name for exponent; indicates the number of repeated multiplications of the base	$2^3=2*2*2=8$
product	something produced by labor or work	result of multiplying two or more quantities together	$6 \times 4 = 24$

References

Dale, E., and J. O'Rourke. 1986. *Vocabulary Building: A Process Approach.* Columbus, OH: Zaner-Bloser.

Stahl, S. A. 1986. "Three Principles of Effective Vocabulary Instruction." *Journal of Reading* 29: 662–668.

———. 1999. *Vocabulary Development: From Reading Research to Practice.* Newton Upper Falls, MA: Brookline Books.

Naming and Knowing Text Features

Successful comprehension depends in part on readers' ability to allocate their limited attention efficiently and effectively to the most relevant pieces of information within the text and within their memory.

—P. van den Broek and K. E. Kremer, "The Mind in Action"

What Are Text Features?

Text features are supports (often visual) that writers use to draw the reader's attention to significant parts of a text to help the reader locate, organize, and learn important information from the text. Text features are also known by several other labels (Herber 1965): adjunct aids, visual aids, graphic support, and text supports, and they can be internal or external text features. In a textbook, internal text features would include such supports as headings, subheadings, boldfaced type, italics, maps, charts, graphs, and so forth. External text features would include supports such as cover material, appendices, glossary, table of contents, index, copyright information, references, and further information. All features help readers locate information efficiently and focus their attention on important information. It is worth noting that text features and text structures are not the same and the terms should not be used interchangeably. Each has its own vocabulary and purpose.

How Could Teaching Text Features Work in the Classroom?

Teaching students about text features will entail several steps: creating an awareness of text features; providing the correct names for the features so that students come to know and use them; and, making sure students use the features for their intended purpose when writing. If your students aren't using any text features when you ask them to write informational texts, they still have not internalized that these are tools writers use to support readers. A generic organizer is provided with text features that could be found in any text regardless of content area. This chart could be used in the instructional sequence that follows.

1. Ask students to create a text features chart or use the generic one found on page A17 in the appendix.
2. Provide student groups with a variety of informational texts.
3. Groups should identify each text feature that is found, create a working definition and purpose for each feature, and include an example (visual, if possible) for the feature. See an example in Figure 1.
4. After all groups have completed charts with the texts they were using, reconvene the class to create common definitions for each.

After students are aware of common text features, you may want to provide students an opportunity to examine text features for a specific type of text or to discover the text features specific to the discipline you are teaching. Emilee Kellermann, a teacher

Figure 1 — Identifying Text Features

Text Feature	Definition/Purpose	Example
• Graph	Visual (diagram) using lines/dots to show change in one or more factors	

Figure 2 — Using Text Features to Find Our Way in Music

Music Feature	Purpose of Text Feature	Information Gained
Title	"Twinkle, Twinkle, Little Star"	a nursery rhyme
Introduction	quarter notes	easy rhythm
Sections	3 sections	The first section is repeated at the end.
Dynamic Markings	mp	The song will be medium soft.
Tempo	gently	not too fast or too slow
Road Map (Any musical signs)	no repeats—a Fermata on last note	can play straight through and hold last note
Hard Measures Rhythm/Melody	big, melodic skip at beginning	easy rhythm and fairly easy melody
Lyrics	about stars	song should be light
History of Song	Song started as a nursery rhyme that many composers have used.	

in the Rockwood, Missouri, school district, generously shared the organizer she developed to help her students learn about text features in music (see Figure 2; a blank version is included on page A18 of the appendix). It is important that students have knowledge of both common text features and the domain-specific features that will be used to study the content in your class.

When and Why Is Teaching Text Features Important?

Most students see the text features as "filler," which is extraneous to what they need to learn from the text. This causes many students to miss important information or get so overwhelmed with the large amount of information, they stop reading. Naming these features provides a domain-specific common language for students to talk about texts they are reading and organize informational texts they are writing in your class. The names of these features will be used in standardized test questions and learning activities for reading, writing, and research. For example, a test question won't ask students to "look at the words under the picture." A more likely question will direct students to examine the caption, key, or legend connected to the picture, map, or graph. Knowing the purpose of these features and how the features can support them when reading and writing will help students develop as efficient and effective learners.

References

Herber, H. L., ed. 1965. *Developing Study Skills in Secondary Schools.* Newark, DE: International Reading Association.

van den Broek, P., and K. E. Kremer. 2000. "The Mind in Action: What It Means to Comprehend During Reading." In *Reading for Meaning: Fostering Comprehension in the Middle Grades,* ed. B. M. Taylor, M. F. Graves, and P. van den Broek. New York: Teachers College Press.

Collecting Topic-Specific Language for Writing

Lists of related words, clusters of words in the same category, are more meaningful to students than words collected at random.

—Thomas Carnicelli, *Words Work*

What Is Topic-Specific Language Collection?

I first realized the importance of topical language collection when I was working with the writing scoring for our state assessment test. While reviewing responses for consistency in scoring, I realized that the writers receiving the lowest scores often lacked the topic-specific language needed to address the prompt. When I returned to my classroom, I began using a variety of strategies to help students develop the habit of collecting topic-specific language to help them with academic writing in their content classes. Two of the activities emerged as ones that students enjoyed and learned from: 3–2–1 Note Taking and Inclusion Brainstorming, which I adapted from Blachowicz's Exclusion Brainstorming technique (1986). Regardless of the activity, the goal is to teach students ways to identify, note, and use topic-specific language in speaking and writing.

How Could Teaching Topic-Specific Language Collection Work in the Classroom?

Topic-specific language collection can take many forms. For example, there are many different types of word walls, but one type of wall that supports learning topic-specific words is a topical word wall. The example on page A19 in the appendix shows a topical word wall for Philbrick's (2000) science fiction novel depicting a dystopian society. (The numbers in parentheses indicate the page number where each word was used in the novel.) Based on the topics studied in your discipline, you can create a temporary word wall that changes with each major unit, text, or topic.

One activity that worked well with my students was using my adaptation of Blachowicz's Exclusion Brainstorming technique. I modified it slightly to focus students' attention specifically on including topic-specific language in their writing. The example shown on page A20 in the appendix could be used as part of a unit on medical mysteries; a blank version can be found on page A21.

- Read an excerpt from *Red Madness: How a Medical Mystery Changed What We Eat* (Jarrow 2014) or any other informational text about medical mysteries.
- Provide students with a word bank containing words they will discuss and choose from to use if writing an article about the Pellagra epidemic.
- After discussion and any further reading or research, students can add other topic-specific words they would need to write a news article.

In future reading during this unit's study or exploration of other topics, you could extend their knowledge of words by using the organizer 3–2–1 Note Taking. The example shown on page A22 in the appendix is based on the first chapter of the biography *The Amazing Harry Kellar: Great American Magician* (Jarrow 2012), and a blank version is on page A23.

- In lengthy reading, students chunk the text and add to the organizer for each section. With short readings, students could complete one section for each reading, noting the title in column 1.
- Students collect three topic-specific words they would need to write about the topic (column 2) and use one or more of the words to note two pieces of information the author would want them to remember about the topic (column 3).
- Finally, students create a title or section heading using one of the words (column 4).
- By the time they finish the text, they have a collection of vocabulary words to write about the topic and a list of the main idea and supporting details for each section.

When and Why Is Teaching Topic-Specific Language Important?

As I mentioned in the introduction, teaching new words and an awareness of language needs to be part of everything we do. Rather than relegating vocabulary instruction to only one time in a day or week, it needs to be at the forefront of all literacy activities. Marzano and Pickering state that "the more terms a person knows about a given subject, the easier it is to understand—and learn—new information related to that subject" (2005, 3). Noting and categorizing new words related to a topic or idea help students develop specificity in thinking, speaking, and writing in all disciplines.

References

Blachowicz, C. L. Z. 1986. "Making Connections: Alternatives to the Vocabulary Notebook." *Journal of Reading* 29 (2): 643–649.

Carnicelli, T. 2001. *Words Work: Activities for Developing Vocabulary, Style, and Critical Thinking*. Portsmouth, NH: Heinemann.

Jarrow, G. 2012. *The Amazing Harry Kellar: Great American Magician*. Honesdale, PA: Calkins Creek.

———. 2014. *Red Madness: How a Medical Mystery Changed What We Eat*. Honesdale, PA: Calkins Creek.

Marzano, R. J., and D. J. Pickering. 2005. *Building Academic Vocabulary: Teacher's Manual*. Alexandria, VA: Association for Supervision and Curriculum Development.

Philbrick, R. 2000. *The Last Book in the Universe*. New York: Scholastic.

Preview/Prediction Vocabulary Guide

Students need time to explore new words, play with them, and connect them to concepts they already know. Words without a meaningful context remain random.
—B. J. Overturf, L. H. Montgomery, and M. H. Smith,
Word Nerds

What Is a Preview/Prediction Vocabulary Guide?

A Preview/Prediction Vocabulary Guide is an organizer that helps students use the features of text to anticipate topic-specific vocabulary when reading disciplinary texts (a blank version is included on page A24 of the appendix). Once students gather the topical words from the features (e.g., headings, subheadings, charts, graphs, captions), they can then use those words to predict the content they are about to read and generate prereading questions based on their discussion of the title and the related topic-specific words.

How Could a Preview/Prediction Vocabulary Guide Work in the Classroom?

As with any strategy, students will need direct instruction and modeling to understand the cognitive process of previewing. In the example below, you should make it clear to students that you are focusing on using both text features and the words associated with those features to anticipate and connect to the content. The completed organizer shown in the figure is an example based on a chapter from *A History of US: From Colonies to Country, 1710–1791* (Hakim 1999). *N/A* is placed in the cells if that feature is not used in the text. When designing your guide, you may want to change the features to match your lesson and the texts you use.

The following steps could be used to model this important strategy:

- Introduce students to the strategy with a hook such as a movie trailer or book cover.
- Use a textbook or other informational text and show students how you would use the guide. If you use a chapter or section they have already read, they will be able to focus more closely on the strategy. Emphasize that you are looking for topic-specific words in the features.
- Provide time for students to practice the strategy in pairs or groups in anticipation of their next reading assignment.
- Bring closure to the lesson by using an exit slip that asks students to summarize the strategy in their own words and reflect on how the strategy could help increase knowledge of words and comprehension.

A24

Preview/Prediction Vocabulary Guide

Preview the chapter by using text features to note domain- and topic-specific words.

Title/Subtitle "A Massacre in Boston"	Headings/Subheadings N/A	Visuals and Captions acting radically colonies massacre preserve rebellion liberties representatives First Continental Congress
Bold, Italicized, Highlighted regiment Loyalists commanding Patriots Whigs, Tories	Repeated Words congress massacre colonies quarter	Introduction/Summary agitator colonies organizer revolution citizen Redcoats quartered, Quartering Act
Review Question Words N/A	Focus Words (sidebar) commanding congress Whigs, Tories, Loyalists, Patriots	Standards or Objectives Words N/A

Use these words to discuss predicted content and develop questions to guide your reading.

Predicted Content	Questions
• Detailed description leading to Boston Massacre • Opinions about who was at fault (politics)	• Who was responsible for the Massacre? • What were the repercussions?

When and Why Should I Use a Preview/Prediction Vocabulary Guide?

Students are most likely to attempt reading a text without taking time to preview it for information or tap into existing knowledge they might have that would help them comprehend what they are about to read. In "The Development of Strategic Readers," Paris, Wasik, and Turner discuss readers who do not employ strategies that would increase their comprehension: "Nonstrategic reading in these situations reflects a mixture of developmental naivete, limited practice, lack of instruction, and motivational reluctance to use unfamiliar or effortful strategies" (1991, 609). While some students know the importance of previewing and choose not to employ the strategy, most students do not know the importance. The use of this strategy is supported by a large body of research that shows instruction in previewing increases student comprehension of both textual and inferential information.

References

Hakim, J. 1999. *A History of US: From Colonies to Country, 1710–1791.* New York: Oxford University Press.

Overturf, B. J., L. H. Montgomery, and M. H. Smith. 2013. *Word Nerds: Teaching All Students to Learn and Love Vocabulary.* Portland, ME: Stenhouse.

Paris, S. G., B. A. Wasik, and J. C. Turner. 1991. "The Development of Strategic Readers." In *Handbook of Reading Research*, vol. 2, ed. R. Barr, M. L. Kamil, P. Mosenthal, and P. D. Pearson. White Plains, NY: Longman.

Word Webs

The semantic mapping procedure is subject to the same cautions as other procedures involving associative networks. Some associative relationships help learning, some interfere. Because semantic mapping is often text based, there is a high chance that the associative relationships will be positive.
—I. S. P. Nation, *Teaching and Learning Vocabulary*

What Are Word Webs?

Word webs are also known as concept webs, semantic webs, or spider maps. They provide students with an opportunity to explore possible connections with words or concepts students will encounter in upcoming reading or in a topic about to be studied. Typically, word web graphic organizers help students define a word based on its characteristics. Regardless of the design, word web organizers generally guide students in answering the following questions:

- What is it?
- What are its characteristics?
- What are examples or nonexamples of the word or concept?

In Figure 1, I highlighted some of the possible categories that can be explored when creating a word web: personal and text connections, word families, antonyms, synonyms, word parts, contexts, and functions. You would never use all categories when creating a word web, but the categories you choose should still lead students to explore or answer the three broad questions.

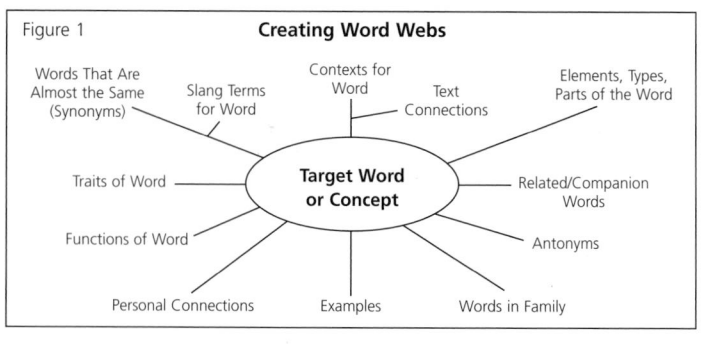

Figure 1 — Creating Word Webs

How Could Word Webs Work in the Classroom?

Word webs would typically be used to explore a major concept, theme, or critical word. The example in Figure 2 is based on Sheinkin's *The Port Chicago 50: Disaster, Mutiny, and the Fight for Civil Rights* (2014). (A blank version is included on page A25 of the appendix.) In this example, I focused on three critical aspects of word analysis: definition derived from context and dictionary; traits and function of the word; and possible uses for the word. When using this type of word web with your students, you will want to decide what its purpose is by asking yourself how important the word or concept is to their overall understanding. Once you decide on the learning outcome, the following instructional actions can make the activity more successful.

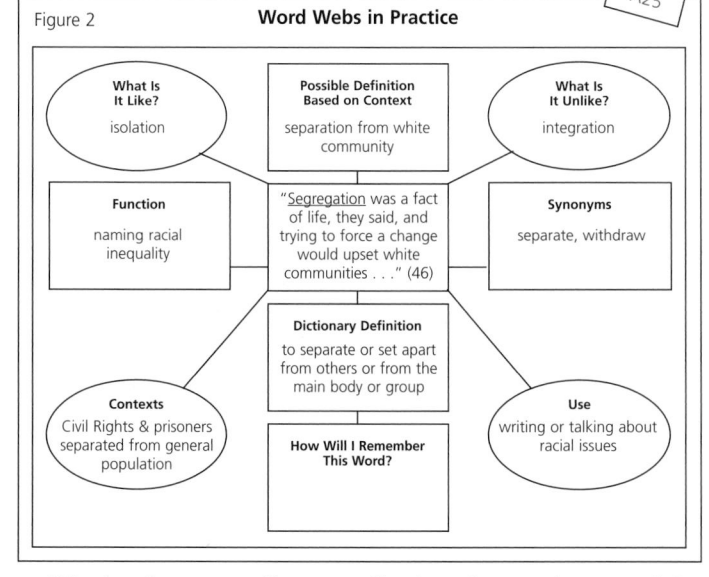

Figure 2 — Word Webs in Practice

- Word webs are usually most effective when students work in small groups to explore the attributes of the word or concept.
- Some of the word web can be explored prior to reading to assess students' current understanding, and the remainder can be completed after encountering the concept in reading or viewing.
- A single word web can be revisited several times to add additional information or deepen understanding.

When and Why Should I Use Word Webs?

You probably won't use a word web to teach a single, passage-critical word; rather, a more likely use will be exploration of major themes or concepts that are multifaceted. Graves noted: "Factors such as how important a word is to understanding a selection students are reading and whether a word represents a central concept in the subject you are teaching are also crucial and often more important than word lists in selecting vocabulary to teach" (2011, 541). The generative nature of a word web in terms of extensions to related words, multiple contexts, and personal use would serve an important role when exploring topic-specific words. For example, if the target word is a topic such as the Holocaust or global warming, many topic-related words will be learned based on their connection to the topic. The ultimate goal is that students will create their own webs to explore words and take notes.

References

Graves, M. F. 2011. "Ask the Expert." *The Reading Teacher* 64 (7): 541.

Nation, I. S. P. 1990. *Teaching & Learning Vocabulary*. Boston, MA: Heinle and Heinle.

Sheinkin, S. 2014. *The Port Chicago 50: Disaster, Mutiny, and the Fight for Civil Rights*. New York: Roaring Book.

Words in Context Plus

Key to this concern is to understand that no formula exists for selecting age-appropriate vocabulary words despite lists that identify "fifth-grade words" or "seventh-grade words." There is simply no basis for determining which words students should be learning at different grade levels.
—I. L. Beck, M. D. McKeown, and L. Kucan, *Bringing Words to Life*

What Is Words in Context Plus?

Words in Context Plus is a word web that supports students in learning an individual word: what it is, what its characteristics are and are not, and what its word families are; a blank version is included on page A26 in the appendix. I had used my original version of a word web, Words in Context (Allen 1999), for many years when I began conducting research in Christine Landaker's middle school social studies classroom. Christine was using a modified version of Words in Context: she eliminated the nonexample category and added categories for noting parts of the word as well as its word families. With these additions, Words in Context Plus became more generative in terms of students learning other words because they were in the word family of the target word. Graves summarizes the research by noting: "Vocabulary instruction is most effective when it is rich, deep, and extended" (2009, 6). Using Words in Context Plus is one way to provide students with "rich, deep, and extended" learning.

How Could Words in Context Plus Work in the Classroom?

When teaching individual words, the sequence of instruction will vary depending on the time you are able to devote and the emphasis the word will require. A typical sequence with the target word *speculated* is outlined here, and a completed organizer is shown in the figure. Italicized words in the figure indicate prereading; nonitalicized words indicate postreading. The example is based on a quote from Murphy's *The Giant and How He Humbugged America* (2012).

- Before reading, display the organizer and provide students with individual copies or ask them to sketch the organizer in their vocabulary notebooks.
- Identify the target word as *speculated*. Give students a short time to discuss the word as it is used in this context.
- If applicable, highlight the parts of the word and brainstorm other words in its family.
- Determine and note a working definition for the word. Note words students come up with in prereading in italics or highlight in some way.
- After reading, return to the organizer and ask students to expand the definition by noting what it is and what it is not. Change cells to match the word (e.g., *can/cannot, would/would not*) if necessary.
- Revisit the organizer when new encounters with the word occur. Bold in the figure indicates a new definition and use of the word.

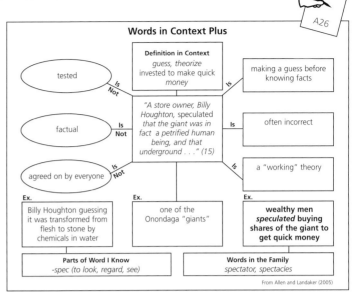

When and Why Should I Use Words in Context Plus?

There are many versions of graphic organizers that help students learn passage-critical words, and they all have a common element: they take time. Words in Context Plus, like many word-exploration organizers, could and should be modified to meet the depth and breadth of word knowledge needed to support comprehension. Graves notes several considerations when deciding how much emphasis (and time) to place on teaching individual words. "It is important to realize that all word-learning tasks are not the same; in fact, the task of learning a word can vary a great deal from one word to another" (2009, 15–16). He notes four criteria when considering how much emphasis and time you would choose to spend on an individual word: conceptual difficulty; students' prior knowledge of the word; how well you want them to know the word; and, what you want them to be able to do with the word.

It is absolutely necessary that individual words be taught as part of any comprehensive vocabulary program. Given time limitations, it is also necessary to make sure the most important words are chosen for in-depth instruction. The rule of thumb for me is deciding if a word is critical to comprehension *and* it will be encountered in other texts and used frequently in other classes and life. If so, this type of organizer will help students develop a deeper knowledge of this high-utility word.

References

Allen, J. 1999. *Words, Words, Words: Teaching Vocabulary in Grades 4–12*. Portland, ME: Stenhouse.

Allen, J., and C. Landaker. 2005. *Reading History: A Practical Guide to Improving Literacy*. New York: Oxford University Press.

Beck, I. L., M. D. McKeown, and L. Kucan. 2002. *Bringing Words to Life: Robust Vocabulary Instruction*. New York: Guilford.

Graves, M. F. 2009. *Teaching Individual Words: One Size Does Not Fit All*. Newark, NJ: The International Reading Association; New York: Teachers College Press.

Murphy, J. 2012. *The Giant and How He Humbugged America*. New York: Scholastic.

Graphically Organized Learning:
Integration, Repetition, and Meaningful Use

Graphic organizers are a step between what the teacher or the text says and what will become long-term memory for the student.

—Marilee Sprenger, *Teaching the Critical Vocabulary of the Common Core*

What Is Graphically Organized Learning?

There are many types of graphic organizers (e. g., chart, diagram, matrix, web), and the use of them has become a very significant part of vocabulary instruction for passage-critical words. Graphic organizers are visual or spatial forms to classify and connect words and ideas. Often, they are used to help students move from an abstract definition to a more concrete application of the word. The overuse of graphic organizers can have the same negative impact as the overuse of sticky notes or work-sheets. However, purposeful use of graphic organizers to help students note the scope of a word can be very beneficial. One of the most significant benefits of using them for vocabulary instruction is that they provide a way for students to revisit the word and add new information as it is encountered. To avoid copying multiple pages, students can keep vocabulary notebooks and sketch the organizer in their notebooks so the information is graphically organized.

How Could Graphically Organized Learning Work in the Classroom?

There are many graphic organizers online and in professional books that are readily available. I have included three examples here, but you will want to adapt or create your own organizers to meet your instructional goals. The reason I chose these three organizers is that each one was created to serve a unique purpose.

- **Beyond Definitions.** I created Beyond Definitions for students to keep track of high-utility words they were learning (see page A27 in the appendix for a blank organizer). My students didn't use the graphic organizer; they used index cards with the word, typical contexts, and word families on the front of the card and notes documenting where or how they encountered or used the word on the back of the card. After reading *Oh, Yikes!* (Masoff 2006) while studying laws and punishments, the class expanded the word *incarcerated* beyond a definition (see figure).

- **"Defining" a Word.** I created "Defining" a Word to use when teaching passage-critical words encountered in the reading of a whole-class text (see page A28 in the appendix for a blank organizer). In the example shown on page A29 of the appendix, I've taken the word *scathing* from *Deadly Invaders* (Grady 2006) and changed the prompts to match the word being defined. Each time we used the organizer, I simply changed the prompts in the cells to match the target word. In this way, students were making connections to the

Beyond Definitions: *incarcerated*

Concept, Term, Word, or Phrase	Usual Context (Often/Always)	Unusual Context (Rarely/Never)
incarcerated "They were called *carcers* (that's where our word 'incarcerated' comes from)." (p. 208)	jails prisons	in-school suspension being grounded
Belongs to this family of words . . .	**I would probably use this word if/when . . .**	
incarceration unincarcerated incarcerator	If I were reading, talking about, or writing about people who are in prison. In *Oh, Yikes!* it says prisons (called carcers) were cages built 12 feet underground.	

text; generating synonyms and antonyms for the target word; and highlighting a context or example for how or why they would use the word.

- **Word Associations.** I created this organizer for students to use with their independent reading (see page A30 for a blank version). Each week, I asked students to highlight one of the words they had encountered in their reading. They chose a word they wanted to remember and made word associations to help them remember the word and the context from their reading. The example shown on page A31 of the appendix is based on a word from Flood's *Cowboy Up!* (2013).

When and Why Should I Use Graphically Organized Learning?

Graphic organizers should be used when visual representation and determining the connections between cells is important. It definitely is not necessary to use a graphic organizer with each new word that is introduced. A well-constructed organizer can be used and revisited many times to extend the initial understanding of a word. Robinson (1998) and many other researchers have highlighted the support graphic organizers can provide for learners. As with any instructional tool, some students benefit more from the use of organizers than others. In my university classes, I always reminded my students that the best graphic organizer is a blank sheet of paper where students are able to make their own connections and extensions to deepen word knowledge. In a perfect scenario, teacher-made graphic organizers should be a stepping stone to independence. With repetition and integration, it is always the goal that students would extend learning to meaningful use of words.

References

Flood, N. B. 2013. *Cowboy Up! Ride the Navajo Rodeo*. Honesdale, PA: WordSong.

Grady, D. 2006. *Deadly Invaders: Virus Outbreaks Around the World from Marburg Fever to Avian Flu*. New York: Macmillan/Kingfisher.

Masoff, J. 2006. *Oh, Yikes! History's Grossest, Wackiest Moments*. New York: Workman.

Robinson, D. H. 1998. "Graphic Organizers as Aids to Text Learning." *Reading Research and Instruction* 37: 85–105.

Sprenger, M. 2013. *Teaching the Critical Vocabulary of the Common Core: 55 Words That Make or Break Student Understanding*. Alexandria, VA: Association for Supervision and Curriculum Development.

Teaching Word-Learning Strategies

With tens of thousands of words to learn, anything we can do to help students become more proficient independent word learners is an absolute necessity.
—M. F. Graves, *The Vocabulary Book*

What Is Strategy Instruction?

A strategy is a plan or series of steps taken to obtain a goal or a desired result. Strategy instruction involves teaching students how to plan for and take the necessary steps to achieve the goal independently. Strategy instruction is based on the gradual release of responsibility model (Pearson and Gallagher 1983), which identifies the following steps:

- Direct instruction and modeling of the strategy
- Guided practice that allows for teacher and peer support and an opportunity to clarify understanding of the steps of the strategy
- Independent use of the strategy to demonstrate competence in knowing the strategy and knowing when and how to use it

Using this model, I added an anticipatory step to the strategy lesson where you pique students' interest in learning the strategy and introduce them to the strategy they are about to learn. See page A32 in the appendix to note the four stages of planning. Each of the word-learning strategies in this section will have an example strategy lesson based on these instructional steps.

Why Is Strategy Instruction Critical for Developing a Rich and Flexible Vocabulary?

Given the limited number of words we can teach students via direct instruction (300–400 per year) and the large number of words students need to learn (3,000–4,000 per year), it is critical that students know strategies for independently learning new words (Nagy and Anderson 1984; Graves 2006). Several word-learning strategies have a strong research base for significantly extending students' vocabularies: using external context clues; learning structural analysis and using word parts to predict meaning (internal context clues); and learning how to use resources such as dictionaries and related reference tools.

Your instructional goals for teaching strategies to your students remain the same regardless of the strategy being taught:

- Knowledge of the strategy and its critical components
- Knowledge of when to use and not to use the strategy to maximize learning a word
- Knowledge of the strengths and limitations of the strategy
- Knowledge of the generative capacity of the strategy in helping learn other words in the future

It is important for students to understand that a combination of strategies is more effective than any one strategy used in isolation. At intervals throughout the year, use the graphic organizer shown in the figure as a way to reinforce the importance of

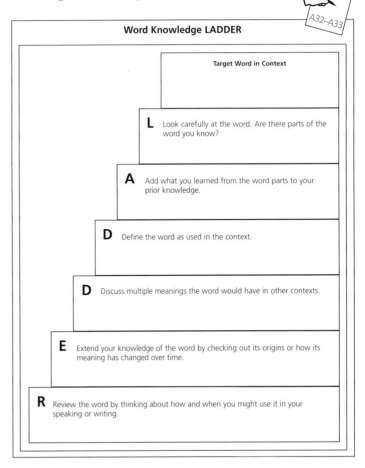

Word Knowledge LADDER

Target Word in Context

L Look carefully at the word. Are there parts of the word you know?

A Add what you learned from the word parts to your prior knowledge.

D Define the word as used in the context.

D Discuss multiple meanings the word would have in other contexts.

E Extend your knowledge of the word by checking out its origins or how its meaning has changed over time.

R Review the word by thinking about how and when you might use it in your speaking or writing.

relying on more than one strategy; I've included a blank version on page A33 of the appendix. Demonstrating these strategies using passages from content textbooks and discipline-based literary and informational texts is critical. For the maximum impact of these word-learning strategies, they should be taught and revisited in every content class so students can see how to employ the strategies across disciplines.

References

Graves, M. F. 2006. *The Vocabulary Book: Learning & Instruction*. New York: Teachers College Press.

Nagy, W. E., and R. C. Anderson. 1984. "How Many Words Are There in Printed School English?" *Reading Research Quarterly* 19: 304–330.

Pearson, P. D., and M. C. Gallagher. 1983. "The Instruction of Reading Comprehension." *Contemporary Educational Psychology* 8: 317–344.

How to Use Internal Context Clues: Prefixes, Root Words, Suffixes

A commonsense approach, and one that benefits children, is to offer a few basics on affixes—and maybe on roots—but mostly to offer lots of good stories about wonderful words. Students have difficulty remembering lists of disconnected words and word parts. They don't forget stories.
—Susan Ohanian, *The Great Word Catalogue*

Why Is It Important to Teach Students How to Use Structural Analysis as a Tool For Learning New Words?

While some would argue about the age when children should be introduced to using structural analysis (word parts) or how those word parts should be taught, few would argue that teaching children that words can be composed of elements is essential knowledge. Dale and O'Rourke stated: "This ability to distinguish word parts is often the chief factor differentiating average students from verbally superior students" (1986, 14). Stahl extended that importance by noting: "This strategy may be especially important for content-area reading, where many of the words contain identifiable word parts whose meanings are the same in many different words" (1999, 44–45). As one part of a repertoire of word-learning strategies, knowledge of the function of prefixes, root words, and suffixes in helping students learn new words is seldom questioned or debated. What is debated is how word parts should be introduced and the relative value of asking students to memorize lists of common prefixes, root words, and suffixes.

How Could I Teach Students to Use Word Parts as *One* Tool for Determining the Meaning of a Word or Phrase?

Teaching students how to use word parts to predict or determine the meaning of a word is a complex task. Many teachers ask students to memorize lists of word parts and definitions, but it is also important to teach them that the definition of these word parts isn't always helpful for learning new words. White, Sowell, and Yanagihara (1989) found that twenty prefixes and suffixes account for 97 percent and 99 percent of affixed words in printed school English. If focusing on word parts, these lists would provide a good *starting* point by working with one affix at a time. One of many excellent resources for common root and affixes can be found at http://www.prefixsuffix.com/rootchart.php.

Introduction/Anticipation

Remind students that when they know parts of words, it sometimes makes learning new words easier. Show them that words can be made up of root or base words, prefixes, and suffixes.

Word Part	Contributes . . .	Example
Root Word	Most of the word's meaning	*Active* means . . .
Prefix	Modification of a word's meaning	Add prefix *in-* (*inactive*). How is meaning changed?
Suffix	Less than root or prefix but can tell us something about how the word is used	Add suffix *–ity* (*inactivity*). How is meaning changed?

Modeled Lesson

Focus on prefixes (or any one of the word parts) and explore functions of the prefix as well as definitions of the most common ones. Provide students with a list of words that would be appropriate for the grade level, and model using a graphic organizer such as the ones shown on page A34 of the appendix. This is also a good time to share words that are inconsistent or misdirective in terms of meaning. A generic organizer, Using Word Parts to Learn New Words, is provided on page A35 in the appendix for use with prefixes, root words, or suffixes.

Guided Learning/Independent Practice

Students should work together to reinforce and practice what you taught in the modeled lesson. Middle school teachers Kim Barnes and Mary Curtis share the guided practice in their classroom.

We put 6 laminated cards (3 yellow; 3 green), 1 expo marker, and a tissue in a one-gallon bag. We also give each student a flipchart with pages allocated for prefixes, root or base words, and suffixes. Each day we start with a word of the day and students have to break down the word into parts and use the expo markers to write them on the yellow cards. Then we ask them to define each part using the green cards. They place the green cards under the yellow cards so they can manipulate the words. We then have a discussion about words with the same prefix, root, or suffix to create word families. They note new information in a flipchart that they keep in their folders for daily use.

Students love activities where they can create new words using the root words and affixes they know. In order for awareness of word parts to become a consistent part of learning new words, it is important for students to create and use a cumulative list of word parts when encountered.

Closure

Use any type of closure that allows for formative assessment to check for understanding and misunderstanding about the concepts taught. For example, you could use the organizer Using Structural Analysis to Predict Meaning (found on page A36 in the appendix) as an exit slip or as a model for students to keep an ongoing list in their academic notebooks. The organizer on page A37 in the appendix shows how, while reading Kroll's *Barbarians!* (2009), students could add new word parts or new information about word parts previously encountered. In subsequent lessons, reinforce concepts by adding to knowledge of noted word part and extending the lesson to additional word parts.

References

Dale, E., and J. O'Rourke. 1986. *Vocabulary Building: A Process Approach*. Columbus, OH: Zaner-Bloser.

Kroll, S. 2009. *Barbarians!* New York: Dutton Children's Books.

Ohanian, S. 2002. *The Great Word Catalogue: FUNdamental Activities for Building Vocabulary*. Portsmouth, NH: Heinemann.

Stahl, S. A. 1999. *Vocabulary Development: From Reading Research to Practice*. Newton Upper Falls, MA: Brookline Books.

White, T. G., J. Sowell, and A. Yanagihara. 1989. "Teaching Elementary Students to Use Word-Part Clues." *The Reading Teacher* 42: 302–309.

How to Use External Context Clues to Learn New Words

Students must know why and when to use context. Sometimes the context is quite explicit about word meanings; at other times the clues given by the author merely suggest an attribute or relationship. Students need to see and discuss various levels of context explicitness to develop sensitivity to the different levels of help context can provide.
—C. Blachowicz and P. J. Fisher, *Teaching Vocabulary in All Classrooms*

Why Is It Important to Teach Students How to Use Context Clues?

Regardless of what content is being assessed on a standardized test, students' strategies for figuring out the meaning of new and unknown words are always being tested. Words have meaning in a context, and research supports direct instruction in showing students how to use those clues from the text in order to help determine word meaning. In order for students to effectively use external (outside the unknown word) context clues, they have to know several things about context:

- Words have meaning in a context and the context can provide clues for meaning.
- Authors provide many types of clues to a word's meaning and knowing where to find and how to identify the clues is critical.
- Context clues, when used alone, can be uninformative or misleading.

Research shows that local context—the rest of the words in the sentence containing the unknown word—when used as the sole source of word meaning, is unreliable (Baumann and Kame'enui 1991). However, when students receive instruction and guided practice in determining word meaning through context and when definitional information is combined with context clues, students are more likely to effectively use context (Stahl and Fairbanks 1986; Nagy 1988). Therefore, it is important to provide students with an opportunity to learn how and when to use context clues. For maximum benefit, this instruction and reinforcement should occur in all content areas.

How Could I Teach Students to Effectively Use Context Clues?

Teaching students how to use context clues is not an easy task regardless of how easy it looks when you use lessons or worksheets where the context explicitly leads students to a word's meaning. While many textbooks offer pronunciation, definition, or example as parenthetical supports for learning content-specific words, most texts students read will not offer such explicit support. Beck, McKeown, and McCaslin (1983) highlight contextual levels of helpfulness for readers: directive, generally directive, nondirective, or misdirective. As you create lessons, you will want to use examples with explicit context clues as well as examples with nonhelpful or even misleading contexts so students learn how to activate other strategies when the context is questionable in terms of support.

Introduction/Anticipation

Use some kind of age-appropriate pictograph or visual puzzle such as the ones drawn by Troy Cunningham on page A38 in the appendix.

Ask students to try to "read" the pictures for you. Students will easily get "pushing the envelope" and may come up with *Death of a Salesman* and *Grapes of Wrath* for the remaining two. Ask them what they used to figure out what the pictures meant. Most students will agree that they used the picture clues with their background knowledge. Explain that when authors write, they expect readers to use their background knowledge with clues in the rest of the sentence surrounding an unknown word in order to figure out what a word means.

Modeled Lesson

Choose excerpts from a variety of texts you use in your class. The excerpts should contain a word students probably do not know, and the contexts should provide varying levels of support. Provide students with a blank Get a Clue! organizer (see page A39 in the appendix). Demonstrate each of the context clue types, and think aloud about how that context could help you determine or predict the meaning of the unknown word. You will want to use only a few types in each lesson and then repeat the lesson several times reinforcing the types previously encountered and introducing a new type. See page A40 in the appendix for descriptions and examples of each type of context clue. All examples came from two informational texts: *Frogs! Strange and Wonderful* (Pringle 2012) and *Scorpions! Strange and Wonderful* (Pringle 2013).

Guided Learning/Independent Practice

Provide students with an opportunity to practice the context types you introduced using the graphic organizer Finding the Clues (see page A41 in the appendix). Provide time for students to work together perusing a variety of texts to find sentences with unknown words and practicing using context clues to help them determine meaning.

Closure

Close the first and subsequent lessons by giving students time to generate the challenges they faced and what other strategies they used when context was confusing or nonhelpful. This can be done using individual or group exit slips, or as paired or whole-group discussion.

After several modeled lessons on where to find context clues and how to use them in order to determine word meaning, students should be ready to transfer this strategy for their independent use and as part of decoding standardized tests.

References

Baumann, J. E., and E. J. Kame'enui. 1991. "Research on Vocabulary Instruction: Ode to Voltaire." In *Handbook of Research on Teaching the English Language Arts*, ed. J. Flood, J. M. Jensen, D. Lapp, and J. R. Squire. New York: Routledge.

Beck, I. L., M. G. McKeown, and E. S. McCaslin. 1983. "All Contexts Are Not Created Equal." *Elementary School Journal* 83: 177–181.

Blachowicz, C., and P. J. Fisher. 2002. *Teaching Vocabulary in All Classrooms*. 2nd ed. Upper Saddle River, NJ: Pearson Education.

Nagy, W. E. 1988. *Teaching Vocabulary to Improve Reading Comprehension*. Newark, DE: International Reading Association.

Pringle, L. 2012. *Frogs! Strange and Wonderful*. Honesdale, PA: Boyds Mills.

———. 2013. *Scorpions! Strange and Wonderful*. Honesdale, PA: Boyds Mills.

Stahl, S. A, and M. M. Fairbanks. 1986. "The Effects of Vocabulary Instruction: A Model-Based Meta-Analysis." *Review of Educational Research* 56 (1): 72–110.

How to Use Resources to Support Learning New Words

So many things have gone out of date. But after all these years, words are still important. Words are still needed by everyone. Words are used to think with, to write with, to dream with, to hope and pray with. And that is why I love the dictionary. It endures. It works. And as you now know, it also changes and grows.

—Andrew Clements, *Frindle*

Why Is It Important to Teach Students How to Use Resources?

You may wonder why we still need to teach students how to use resources for learning words since most students learned these skills in elementary classes. However, if you have read the Common Core State Standards (2010), you will note that there is a Language standard for use of resources beginning with grade two and up through grade twelve. There are many types of resources students need to know how to use in order to confirm, clarify, extend, or learn the definition of a word. Stahl and Fairbanks (1986) found that a combination of definitional and contextual approaches is more effective than either approach used in isolation. Each approach informs the other. If students are to employ strategies for learning new words from context and definitions, they need to know how to use resources that will help them access those definitions.

How Could I Teach Students to Effectively Use Resources?

Most teachers share the common experience of asking students to look words up in the dictionary. A common response is usually "Which definition should I copy?" or "Can we just write down the first or shortest definition?" Regardless of the strategy lesson for teaching students how to optimally use a dictionary, it should include ways for students to see all that the dictionary offers in terms of information. The lesson components for teaching students how to use a dictionary could include the following steps and would need to be repeated with other resources such as a thesaurus or specialized dictionary.

Introduction/Anticipation

Anticipate the strategy lesson with a dictionary-related read-aloud from Clements's *Frindle* (1986) or Salinger's *Well-Defined Vocabulary in Rhyme* (2009). Discuss difficulties you've noticed when asking students to consult a dictionary.

Modeled Lesson

Display one or more words, for example, *combs*, *squeak*, and *grazed*, and think aloud as you predict what these words might mean. Then, add the sentence from *Call of the Klondike: A True Gold Rush Adventure* (Meissner and Richardson 2013) where these words are encountered: "It was simply grand our boats were tossed around like matches in the great *combs* of the rapids; but outside of a thorough wetting and a narrow *squeak* as we *grazed* a rock . . ." (64). Finally, display the information supplied by the dictionary and discuss each of the additional pieces of information you discovered and how that information helped you clarify the meaning of the word as it was used in that context.

Guided Learning/Independent Practice

Provide students with a list of words, and ask them to use the process you modeled to predict the meaning of each word using their background knowledge. Then, add to the predicted meaning by using the context. Finally, gain further confirming or clarifying information using a dictionary. See an example using Meissner and Richardson's *Call of the Klondike: A True Gold Rush Adventure* (2013) in the following figure; a blank version is included on page A42 in the appendix.

Expanding Definitions

Background Knowledge: Discuss the following words and make a prediction about what you think these words mean based on your background knowledge.

arduous	passes	bustling
stampeders	series	swooped
gear	depressed	entrepreneurs

Context Clues: Read the following passage where the words above appear in an informational text, *Call of the Klondike: A True Gold Rush Adventure*. Discuss the words in context and add information about each word's meaning based on the new information you gain from the context.

The journey there would be long and arduous, as gold seekers would soon find out. To reach Dawson City, most stampeders would travel by steamship to Alaska, haul gear over steep mountain passes into Canada, and then travel more than five hundred miles by boat down a series of lakes and rivers.

Most stampeders left for the Klondike from Seattle, which quickly transformed from an economically depressed city into a bustling port. Prospectors swooped into stores and bought thousands of dollars' worth of goods. Every store seemed to advertise Klondike gold rush supplies, whether it was boots, guns, sleds, beans, or "special" Klondike underwear. Some Seattle entrepreneurs even advertised regular dogs as sled dogs that could pull heavy loads across snowfields and up frozen rivers. (2013, 16)

Closure

Use the graphic organizers shown on pages A43 and A44 of the appendix to close the lesson (blank versions can be found on pages A45 and A46). These can be used as group or individual exit slips or to support students in noting in their academic notebooks the text features of dictionaries and how those features could help them independently learn new words.

References

Clements, A. 1996. *Frindle*. New York: Aladdin Paperbacks.

Meissner, D., and K. Richardson. 2013. *Call of the Klondike: A True Gold Rush Adventure*. Honesdale, PA: Calkins Creek.

National Governors Association (NGA) Center for Best Practices, Council of Chief State School Officers (CCSSO). 2010. Common Core State Standards. Washington, DC: NGA/CCSSO.

Salinger, M. 2009. *Well-Defined Vocabulary in Rhyme*. Honesdale, PA: Boyds Mills.

Stahl, S. A., and M. M. Fairbanks. 1986. "The Effects of Vocabulary Instruction: A Model-Based Meta-Analysis." *Review of Educational Research* 56 (1): 72–110.

Fostering Word Consciousness

Now Jip was just an ignorant boy and it wasn't his business, he knew, to try to tell a writer how to write a book, but it stood to reason that if you want to catch a reader tight, the trap needs to be plain and strong with no smell of the trapper lingering on it.

—Katherine Paterson, *Jip: His Story*

What Is Word Consciousness?

Graves defines word consciousness as "*awareness of* and *interest in* words and their meanings" (2006, 119). Word-conscious students display a wide variety of characteristics that fall under the umbrella of awareness and interest. A few of these characteristics are listed here:

- They find words interesting. They may like the way a word sounds or be fascinated with the origin of a word.
- They enjoy word play. They may enjoy using words in interesting ways and notice when others do as well.
- They are willing to take risks with words. They may have seen a word but never heard it pronounced and are willing to try using it in their speaking. They are confident in trying to assimilate interesting words into their own speaking. For example, one of my students said a group of kids who were listening to a conversation wouldn't be in trouble if they hadn't been "earsdropping." One of Kyle Gonzalez's students said he would like to "diaphragm" that sentence.
- They know a lot of words and enjoy being able to play or banter with those words.
- They understand that language is power. As a result they are conscious of the language used when speakers are using words to persuade or manipulate.
- They are always learning new words and new ways to use those words.
- They enjoy inventing language if no "appropriate" word exists.

How Can Word Consciousness Become a Part of Vocabulary Instruction?

The range of activities that foster word consciousness is limited only by your imagination. When students see that you value words and word play, they will become motivated to participate. Blachowicz and Fisher (2004) provide educators with a research base as well as tools and activities to "keep the 'fun' in fundamental," and a quick Internet search will give you access to a world of word-consciousness activities that provide engaging cognitive tasks to increase awareness and use of words. If you haven't discovered www.alphadictionary.com, you will want to make that a frequent site for you and your students.

You may be thinking that you have so much content to address that there isn't time for activities that foster word consciousness, but many activities can be created to support learning in your discipline. Researching eponyms (words derived from a person's name or place) can result in increasing students' knowledge of history or science as they connect words to names and places. Giving students an opportunity to research the origin of words used in your discipline can give them a meaningful connection or story to help them remember the words. Word-consciousness activities can be used as admit or exit slips, energy boosts, or knowledge quests. The examples I use in this section focus on arrays of language (both linear and hierarchical), language precision, language register, and identification of collective nouns. Regardless of when and how you weave word-consciousness activities into your curriculum, you will notice a significant change in students' awareness, engagement, and use of new and interesting words.

References

Blachowicz, C. L. Z., and P. Fisher. 2004. "Keep the 'Fun' in Fundamental: Encouraging Word Awareness and Incidental Word Learning in the Classroom Through Word Play." In *Vocabulary Instruction: Research to Practice*, ed. J. F. Baumann and E. J. Kame'enui. New York: Guilford.

Graves, M. F. 2006. *The Vocabulary Book: Learning & Instruction*. New York: Teachers College Press.

Paterson, K. 1998. *Jip: His Story*. New York: Puffin Books.

Using the Just-Right Word: Arrays of Word Meanings

A47–A48

Teachers can help students grow in semantic skill by helping them associate what they already know with what they are learning. The best approach in teaching vocabulary is to get students to classify new words and to make finer discriminations about words they already know.
—E. Dale and J. O'Rourke, *Vocabulary Building*

What Are Arrays of Word Meanings?

Many different types of activities focused on language subtleties are used in all content classrooms to help students choose the "just-right" word in their speaking and writing. Hierarchical or Linear Arrays, Semantic Gradients (Blachowicz and Fisher 2006), and Semantic Scales (McKenna 2002) are just a few of the types of arrays being used to help students integrate new words for known concepts.

* **Hierarchical Arrays.** These arrays require students to arrange words into graded order or rank. Examples of hierarchical arrays could include the order of offices in government, ranks in academia or military, or taxonomy in biology.
* **Linear Arrays, Semantic Gradients, Semantic Scales.** These types of arrays are all based on degree or shades of meaning. You can provide students with words to place in ascending or descending order or you can ask students to generate words. In either case, most teachers provide a closed array with antonymous ends to anchor students' development of words that fit between the ends, for example, *aggravating . . . pleasing; horrific . . . soothing; lazy . . . industrious.*

How Could Arrays Work in the Classroom?

Students and teachers love working with language arrays; they are easy to create, and the benefit in terms of adding new words to students' existing lexicons is immediate. While students might not know an exact definition for a word, they will often know that it is less than or greater than another word. A graphic organizer such as the one shown in the figure can be used for generation of words and discussion. After generating the words, students then sort them in gradations that name relationships. This type of activity generates a lot of very productive talk.

I find the most effective way to do an array activity is to use teacher-generated words cards that students can sort. For example, I created distance word cards for teachers and students who were reading the informational text *When Elephants Fight* (Walters and Bradbury 2008). The five chapters detail the lives of children in war-torn countries who had to go long distances to migrate to refugee camps or other villages, so I created word cards

with each card containing a word or phrase that named distance (e.g., *kilometer, yard, inch, a stone's throw, centimeter,* etc.)

Prior to reading the book, students are involved in an array activity to develop awareness of a variety of distance words. A sequence for the activity follows.

* One distance word is written on each word card.
* Students work in small groups to put the words they know in order from least to greatest distance.
* Students then try to guess where the unknown words might be placed on the array they have started.
* Students check definitions using dictionaries and the glossary to help them reorder the words, if necessary.
* Finally, blank cards can be given to students so they can add any distance words that aren't in the array.

After the array is completed, we preview the book using the text features, and anticipate the content of the book based on the information gained from the array and previewing activities. The visual and kinesthetic activities allow students to develop a sense of the challenges these children faced. In addition, knowing some of the distance words prior to reading the text supports deeper comprehension while reading.

In anticipation of discussing and writing about characters in ELA, I offer students an array of words that could describe characters: *bothersome, grouchy, friendly, repugnant, sympathetic, congenial, offensive, grumbling, vexing,* and so on. I provide them with paint chips (readily available at stores with each season's changes in color) and ask them to discuss, order, and note the words on paint chips to indicate negative to positive attributes. The paint-chip activity can be extended with character analysis as shown on page A47 of the appendix, where students discuss characters in *Lay That Trumpet in Our Hands* (McCarthy 2003); a blank version of this organizer is included on page A48. Both activities can be saved and added to throughout the reading of the novel and the writing of character analyses.

When and Why Should I Use Arrays?

One of the most important reasons to use arrays with your students is engagement. The volume of discussion about subtle distinctions between words as students work on an array is amazing to witness. You will hear laughter, debate, and thoughtful arguments about words and the subtleties of language. Not only is this activity engaging but it also provides all three of the principles of effective vocabulary instruction: integration, repetition, and meaningful use (Stahl 1986).

Using the Just-Right Word

Brainstorm words that can describe relationships. A beginning list is started; talk with the members of your group to generate at least 10 more words.

Companion
Friend
Acquaintance
Life partner
Lover
Relative

Stranger |—————————————————————————| Soul mate

Now, use the linear array line above to order your words by degree of relationship. A stranger would be the most-distant relationship and a soul mate the closest relationship. Place your words on the line from least to most significant.

References

Blachowicz, C., and P. Fisher. 2006. *Teaching Vocabulary in All Classrooms.* 3rd ed. Upper Saddle River, NJ: Pearson Education.

Dale, E., and J. O'Rourke. 1986. V*ocabulary Building: A Process Approach.* Columbus, OH: Zaner-Bloser.

McCarthy, S. C. 2003. *Lay That Trumpet in our Hands.* New York: Bantam.

McKenna, M. C. 2002. *Help for Struggling Readers: Strategies for Grades 3–8.* New York: Guilford.

Stahl, S. 1986. "Three Principles of Effective Vocabulary Instruction." *Journal of Reading* 29: 662–668.

Walters, E., and A. Bradbury. 2008. *When Elephants Fight.* Custer, WA: Orca.

Word-Rich Instruction

Rich instruction is very open-ended; it is not some particular set of activities but rather any activity that gets students to use, think about, and become involved with words. The major concept is to provoke thought.
—M. D. McKeown and I. L. Beck, "Direct and Rich Vocabulary Instruction"

What Is Word-Rich Instruction?

As McKeown and Beck note, rich instruction is open ended. While each teacher might develop very different strategies for enriching all components of a comprehensive vocabulary program, the common denominator will be that students will experience an enriched environment where they are immersed in interesting language. They will learn in classrooms filled with texts that use language in ways that make students want to read one book after another. They will learn from teachers who enjoy language, and they will want to emulate that language.

How Could Word-Rich Instruction Work in the Classroom?

Unlike the other specific activities and strategies highlighted in this text, there is no formula for what word-rich instruction might look like in your classroom. Some examples of activities that help create word-rich environments follow.

- Begin class some days with word or critical thinking puzzles. While you won't find this type of activity in state standards documents, it is amazing to see how those three or four minutes can take students from lethargic to energetic. Puzzles can be found in lateral-thinking books, on the Internet, and from companies such as www.mindware.com. They will highlight interesting ways to help students become intrigued with words and learn mnemonic devices for remembering words. For example, you might ask your students what the following words have in common: *banana, dresser, grammar, potato, revive, uneven, voodoo, assess.* Or, ask them to interpret these mnemonic devices: "Please Excuse My Dear Aunt Sally" (order of operations in math); "Kids Prefer Cheese Over Fried Green Spinach" (order of taxonomy in biology); or, "Now I Need a Verse Recalling Pi" (a way to remember the first six digits of Pi).
- Begin some days with definition poetry such as those you would find in Michael Salinger's *Well-Defined Vocabulary in Rhyme* (2009), and ask students to write their own definition poems for general academic or domain-specific vocabulary words.
- Show clips of speeches, talk shows, or news reports, and give students the opportunity to identify propaganda techniques as elements of persuasion: simplification, fallacy, ambiguous words, emotional appeal, hot/cold words, innuendo, exaggeration, bandwagon, and double talk.
- Develop lessons focused on language register. In the activity Whose Talk? Understanding Language Register (see page A49 of the appendix), students are challenged to identify street talk or slang, define the words or phrases, translate the words into Standard English, and identify contexts for both types of language. The example in the figure is based on language used in Aronson and Smith's *Pick-Up Game*

Whose Talk? *Pick-Up Game*			
Street Talk or Slang	Definition	Standard English	Context for Use
front us/fronting	an advance of money before anything else can happen	Provide some up-front capital as an investment.	If I'm hanging out with a friend and he wants us to do something, we would ask him to front us. If I want investors like on Shark Tank, I would ask for up-front capital as an investment against profit.
sweeten the pot run-mouth dude chick skinhead "bumped out" clocked			

(2011). Use informal language from any text as an introductory activity to segue into changing language register for audience and purpose in writing and speaking.

- Create language activities for student collaboration and friendly competition. Students are always more engaged with language activities that offer time to talk and create challenges for other students. Teaching collective nouns with an activity such as A Pod of Dolphins? is one example of an interesting way to study grammar and usage. A sample version is on page A50 of the appendix, and a blank version appears on page A51. This activity can be extended to a lesson on single and plural nouns and subject-verb agreement.

When and Why Should I Use Word-Rich Instruction?

Word-rich instruction is a significant part of fostering word consciousness. It can be a natural part of all that you do, and it can also be planned as support for your instruction. As students become more interested in language, you will find that you won't have to plan as many activities as they will be providing much of the enriched language use in the classroom. McKeown and Beck continue their support of rich instruction with these words: "Give students a variety of information—examples, contexts, pictures, relationships. Then have them engage in interactions—create contexts, compare features of words, explain their reasoning, and discuss meanings and uses" (2004, 21). Fostering word consciousness in these ways forms the foundation for learning all types of academic language.

*Did you figure it out? Move the first letter of each word to the end of the word and you have the same word when read in reverse (e.g., *banana—ananab*).

References

Aronson, M., and C. R. Smith. 2011. *Pick-Up Game: A Full Day of Full Court.* Somerville, MA: Candlewick.

McKeown, M. D., and I. L. Beck. 2004. "Direct and Rich Vocabulary Instruction." In *Vocabulary Instruction: Research to Practice*, ed. J. F. Baumann, and E. J. Kame'enui. New York: Guilford.

Salinger, M. 2009. *Well-Defined Vocabulary in Rhyme.* Honesdale, PA: Boyds Mills.

Four Components of a Comprehensive Vocabulary Program

Providing Rich and Varied Language Experiences	**Teaching Individual Words**
Teaching Word-Learning Strategies	**Fostering Word Consciousness**

Tools for Teaching Academic Vocabulary by Janet Allen. Copyright © 2014. Stenhouse Publishers. All rights reserved.

Read, Reflect, Respond, & Remember

Name _____ Date _____

Title of Book _____ Author _____

My Word of the Day:

I choose this text because . . .

I thought I would learn/enjoy . . .

The text caught my attention because . . .

I questioned . . .

A connection I made when reading this book was . . .

Now, I'd like to read more or talk with someone about . . .

Draw a graphic (pictograph, picture, graphic organizer, image collage) that represents what you want to remember from this reading. Illustrate how your word of the day connects to the reading.

Tools for Teaching Academic Vocabulary by Janet Allen. Copyright © 2014. Stenhouse Publishers. All rights reserved.

Read, Reflect, Respond, & Remember

Name_____ **Date**_____

Title of Book_Mysterious Patterns: Finding Fractals in Nature_____ **Author**_Sarah C. Campbell_

My Word of the Day:
fractal

I choose this text because . . .

When people talk about fractals, I don't really know what they are talking about.

I thought I would learn/enjoy . . .

What fractals are and studying the pictures and drawings.

The text caught my attention because . . .
of the art on the cover

I questioned . . .
what fractals were and tried to figure out why some things are fractals and others aren't.

A connection I made when reading this book was . . .
I used to draw shapes with repeating patterns but didn't know there was a name for that.

Now, I'd like to read more or talk with someone about . . .
Shapes that are fractals and shapes that are not.

Draw a graphic (pictograph, picture, graphic organizer, image collage) that represents what you want to remember from this reading. Illustrate how your word of the day connects to the reading.

I want to remember that fractals are natural shapes with smaller parts that look like the whole shape.

Tools for Teaching Academic Vocabulary by Janet Allen. Copyright © 2014. Stenhouse Publishers. All rights reserved.

Word Talk with Word Questioning

- How are _____ , _____ ,

  _____ , and _____ related?

- What possible connection could there be between _____

  and _____ ?

- What is the relationship between _____

  and _____ ? (Choose seemingly unrelated items.)

- How are _____ , _____ ,

  _____ , and _____

  all related to _____ ?

- If I discovered _____ , why

  wouldn't I be in _____ ?

Tools for Teaching Academic Vocabulary by Janet Allen. Copyright © 2014. Stenhouse Publishers. All rights reserved.

Tools for Teaching Academic Vocabulary by Janet Allen. Copyright © 2014. Stenhouse Publishers. All rights reserved.

Words from the Inside Out

A–B	C–D	E–F	G–H
I–J	K–L	M–N	O–P
Q–R	S–T	U–V	WXYZ

Tools for Teaching Academic Vocabulary by Janet Allen. Copyright © 2014. Stenhouse Publishers. All rights reserved.

5 W's and H of Knowing a Word

?	**Who**	Who would be mostly likely to use this word?
?	**What**	What other words are in this word's family? What else could this word mean?
?	**When**	When would you be most likely to use this word?
?	**Where**	Where did this word originate?
?	**Why**	Why would you choose this word rather than a similar or synonymous word?
?	**How**	How will you remember this word?

Tools for Teaching Academic Vocabulary by Janet Allen. Copyright © 2014. Stenhouse Publishers. All rights reserved.

5 W's and H of Knowing a Word

?	Who	
?	What	
?	When	
?	Where	
?	Why	
?	How	

Tools for Teaching Academic Vocabulary by Janet Allen. Copyright © 2014. Stenhouse Publishers. All rights reserved.

5 W's and H of Knowing a Word: *Interpret*

?	**Who**	Who would be the teacher who would mostly likely use this word?
?	**What**	What would you be expected to do if you were asked to "interpret" something?
?	**When**	When this word is part of a task, what would be a likely context or setting?
?	**Where**	Where did this word originate?
?	**Why**	Why might you confuse this word with *analyze, describe,* or *summarize*?
?	**How**	How is this word defined? How will you remember its meaning?

Tools for Teaching Academic Vocabulary by Janet Allen. Copyright © 2014. Stenhouse Publishers. All rights reserved.

Tools for Teaching Academic Vocabulary by Janet Allen. Copyright © 2014. Stenhouse Publishers. All rights reserved.

Comparison by Analysis

General Academic Vocabulary	Definition	Unique Characteristics	In my own words, this means I'm being asked to . . . .

Summarize your conclusions about similarities and differences between and among the academic vocabulary words in this cluster.

Tools for Teaching Academic Vocabulary by Janet Allen. Copyright © 2014. Stenhouse Publishers. All rights reserved.

Word Logs

	A	
controlled experiment **C** constant	dependent variable **D**	
encounter **E** Earth science	**F**	

B J

Science- is a way to learn more about the natural world.

Theory- explanation of things or events that is based on knowlegde gained from many obser vations and explerements.

Scientific theory- an attempt to explain a pattern observed reapetedly in the natrual world.

Scientific law- A role that describes a pattern in nature.

System- a collection of Structures, cycles, and processes that relate to and interact with each other.

Life Science- the Study of living things and how they interact.

Earth Science- the Study of Earth's Systems and Systems in space.

Physical Science- the Study of matter and energy.

Technology- is the practical use of Science or applied Science.

Tools for Teaching Academic Vocabulary by Janet Allen. Copyright © 2014. Stenhouse Publishers. All rights reserved.

Collaborate for Understanding: Think-Pair-Share

Target Word

Think/Write about your understanding of the word.

Pair with someone to describe, explain, or compare your understandings of the word.

Share your knowledge of the word by creating a visual to share or dramatizing the word in order to teach the word to others.

Tools for Teaching Academic Vocabulary by Janet Allen. Copyright © 2014. Stenhouse Publishers. All rights reserved.

Word Logs

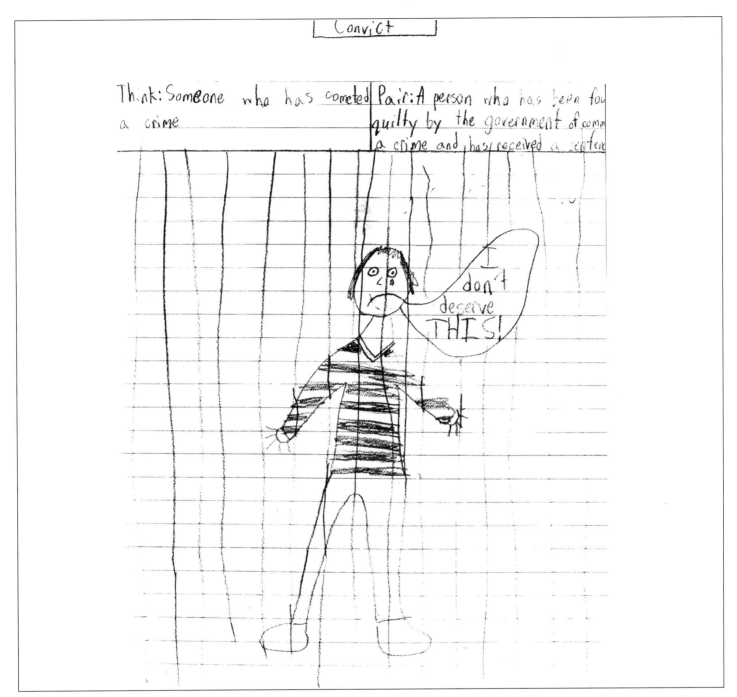

Convict

Think: Someone who has cometed a crime

Pair: A person who has been fou guilty by the government of comm a crime and has received a senten

I don't deserve THIS!

Tools for Teaching Academic Vocabulary by Janet Allen. Copyright © 2014. Stenhouse Publishers. All rights reserved.

Tools for Teaching Academic Vocabulary by Janet Allen. Copyright © 2014. Stenhouse Publishers. All rights reserved.

Portable Word Wall for _____

A–B	C–D	E–F	G–H
I–J	K–L	M–N	O–P
Q–R	S–T	U–V	WXYZ

Word Notes:

Tools for Teaching Academic Vocabulary by Janet Allen. Copyright © 2014. Stenhouse Publishers. All rights reserved.

Academic Vocabulary Cards

Information from the Teacher (Definition, Context, Examples)	Restate in My Own Words

Additional Information from Reading or Viewing	Mnemonic to Help Me Remember (Visual, Jingle)

Tools for Teaching Academic Vocabulary by Janet Allen. Copyright © 2014. Stenhouse Publishers. All rights reserved.

Word Logs

Tools for Teaching Academic Vocabulary by Janet Allen. Copyright © 2014, Stenhouse Publishers. All rights reserved.

Information

智能=Infer

In this book we had to infer to know who was the person who shot Mr. Hirsh

INFER

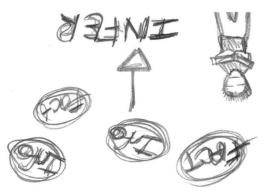

fact The fact fact

Infer

information I know + new information with new information = conclusion

when we see a mystery movie we have to infer to know who the murder was or who is the next victim

Expert Language

Word	What I already know about this word . . .	In this class, it means . . .	Visual to help me remember . . .

Tools for Teaching Academic Vocabulary by Janet Allen. Copyright © 2014. Stenhouse Publishers. All rights reserved.

Identifying Text Features

Text Feature	Definition/Purpose	Example
• Graph		
• Tables		
• Headings		
• Subheadings		
• Titles		
• Text boxes		
• Inset boxes		
• Table of contents		
• Index		
• Glossary		
• Labels		
• Keys/legends		
• Captions		
• Photographs		
• Illustrations		
• Fact boxes		
• Questions		
• Objectives		
• Vocabulary		
• Diagrams		
• Introductions		
• Summary statements		
• Review questions		
• Maps		
• Other		

Tools for Teaching Academic Vocabulary by Janet Allen. Copyright © 2014. Stenhouse Publishers. All rights reserved.

Using Text Features to Find Our Way in Music

Music Feature	Purpose of Text Feature	Information Gained
Title		
Introduction		
Sections		
Dynamic Markings		
Tempo		
Road Map (Any musical signs)		
Hard Measures Rhythm/Melody		
Lyrics		
History of Song		

Tools for Teaching Academic Vocabulary by Janet Allen. Copyright © 2014. Stenhouse Publishers. All rights reserved.

Tools for Teaching Academic Vocabulary by Janet Allen. Copyright © 2014, Stenhouse Publishers. All rights reserved.

Portable Word Wall: *The Last Book in the Universe*

New Words

mindprobe (7)
trendies (7)
latch (8)

Old Words/New Use

mope (7)
wheel (8)
gummy (8)

Science Language

needlebrains (10)
suicidal mope (14)
long-term memory (16)

Environmental Words

Eden (7)
Urb (10)
Big Shake (10)

Language of the Future

total mind melt (7)
voicewriter (7)
family unit (8)
stackbox (10)
backtimer (10)
latchboss (10)

Slang

"bust him down" (9)
'boxers (11)

Tools for Teaching Academic Vocabulary by Janet Allen. Copyright © 2014, Stenhouse Publishers. All rights reserved.

Inclusion Brainstorming: *Pellagra*

Discuss these words with members of your group. Take on the role of a news reporter writing about this mysterious disease. Decide which words you would include in your article. Exclude words you would not use; add additional topic-related words you would need for the article.

desperate	blisters	poisoning
hemorrhage	cancer	rash
scavengers	prove	efficient
unemployed	dreaded	government
scabs	minor	appropriate
scraps	rations	developed
marriage	rats	diarrhea

Based on your group discussion, what other critical words would you now add to the ones you chose from the list above?

Adapted from Blachowicz (1986)

Tools for Teaching Academic Vocabulary by Janet Allen. Copyright © 2014. Stenhouse Publishers. All rights reserved.

Inclusion Brainstorming

Discuss the words with members of your group. Take on the role of a news reporter and decide which of these words you would use in your article about this event and which you would exclude from your article.

Based on your group discussion, what other critical words would you now add to the ones you chose from the list above?

_____   _____

_____   _____

_____   _____

Adapted from Blachowicz (1986)

Tools for Teaching Academic Vocabulary by Janet Allen. Copyright © 2014. Stenhouse Publishers. All rights reserved.

3–2–1 Note Taking

Keeping a record of what stands out for you as you read can help you when writing about a text. Use this organizer to note significant words and notes. Then, summarize your reading by creating chapter titles (or section headings) that highlight the most important points in your reading.

Chapter or Section #	List 3 important words related to the topic.	Use one or more of the words to note 2 things the author would want you to remember.	Write a chapter title or section heading that includes 1 of your words.
"The Magic Posters"	illusion superstition devils/imps	1. Poster featured an illusion from his show. 2. Used devils to make tricks seem more mysterious.	*"Join These Devils for a Night to Remember"*

Tools for Teaching Academic Vocabulary by Janet Allen. Copyright © 2014. Stenhouse Publishers. All rights reserved.

3–2–1 Note Taking

Keeping a record of what stands out for you as you read can help you when writing about a text. Use this organizer to note significant words and notes. Then, summarize your reading by creating chapter titles (or section headings) that highlight the most important points in your reading.

Chapter or Section #	List 3 important words related to the topic.	Use one or more of the words to note 2 things the author would want you to remember.	Write a chapter title or section heading that includes 1 of your words.

Tools for Teaching Academic Vocabulary by Janet Allen. Copyright © 2014. Stenhouse Publishers. All rights reserved.

Preview/Prediction Vocabulary Guide

Preview the chapter by using text features to note domain- and topic-specific words.

Title/Subtlte	Headings/Subheadings	Visuals and Captions
Bold, Italicized, Highlighted	**Repeated Words**	**Introduction/Summary**
Review Question Words	**Focus Words (sidebar)**	**Standards or Objectives Words**

Use these words to discuss predicted content and develop questions to guide your reading.

Predicted Content	Questions
• • •	• • •

Tools for Teaching Academic Vocabulary by Janet Allen. Copyright © 2014. Stenhouse Publishers. All rights reserved.

Word Webs in Practice

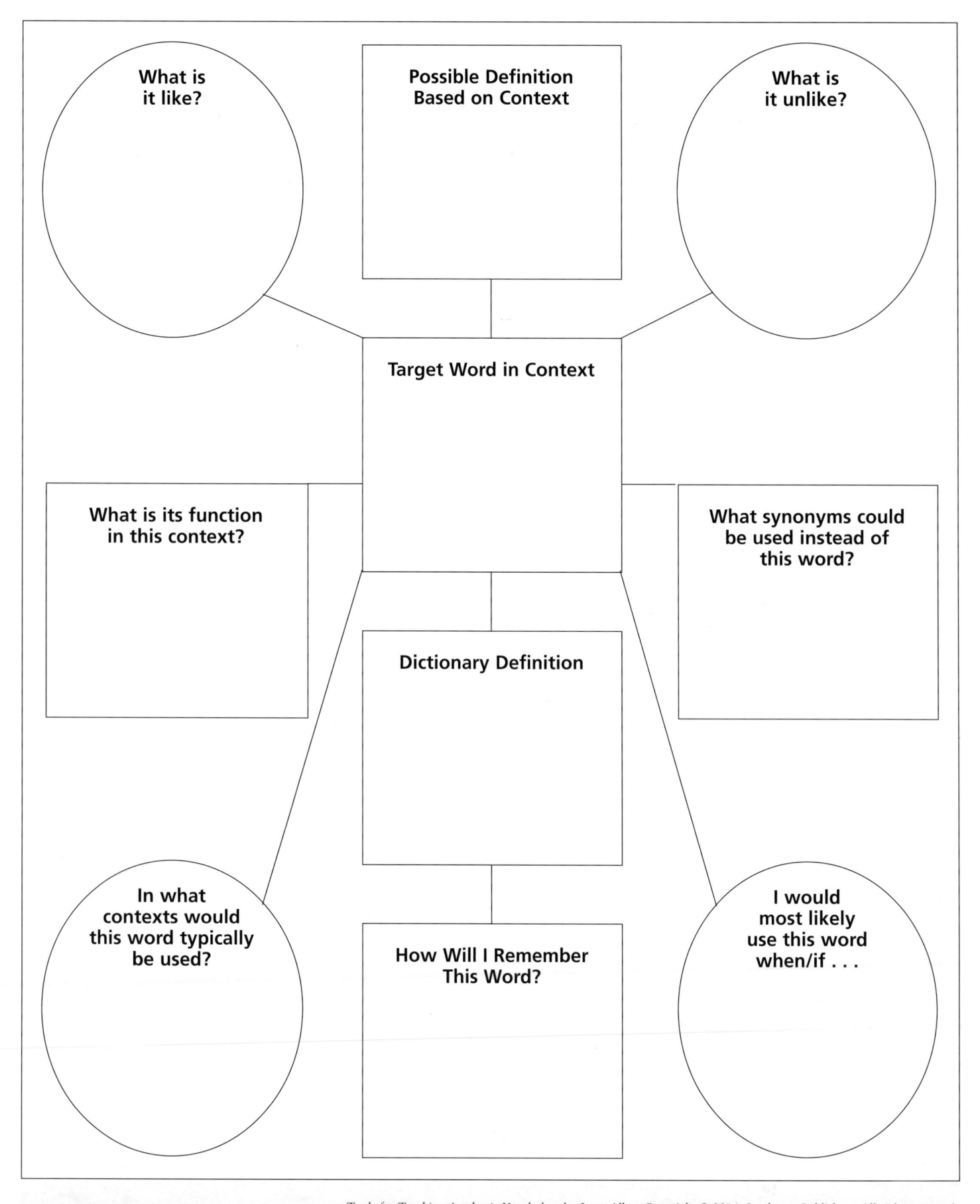

What is it like?

Possible Definition Based on Context

What is it unlike?

Target Word in Context

What is its function in this context?

What synonyms could be used instead of this word?

Dictionary Definition

In what contexts would this word typically be used?

How Will I Remember This Word?

I would most likely use this word when/if . . .

Tools for Teaching Academic Vocabulary by Janet Allen. Copyright © 2014. Stenhouse Publishers. All rights reserved.

Words in Context Plus

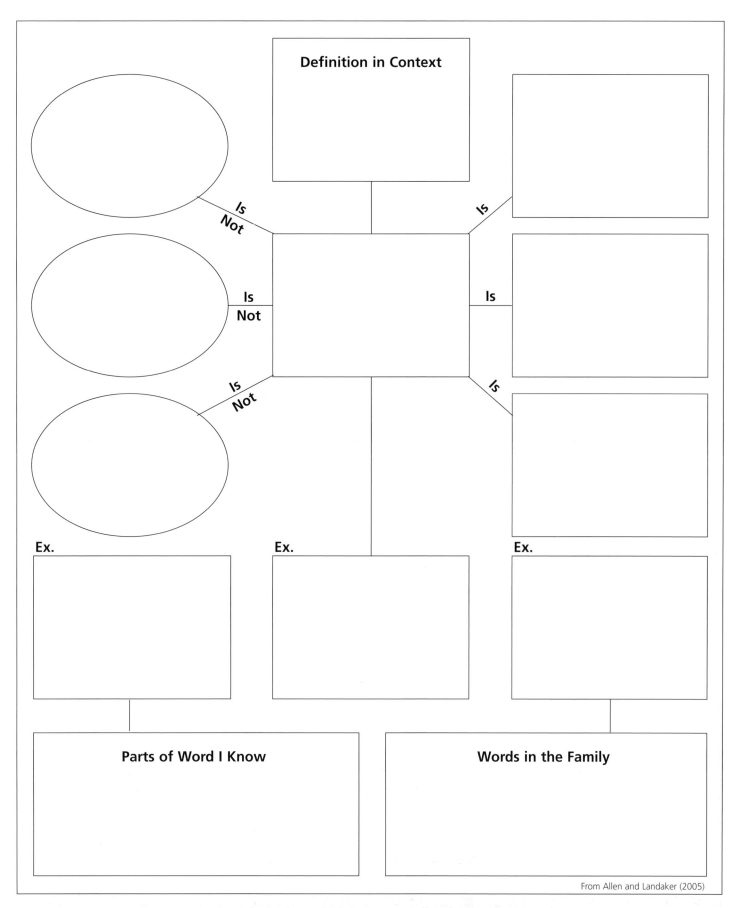

Definition in Context

Is Not

Is Not

Is Not

Is

Is

Is

Ex.

Ex.

Ex.

Parts of Word I Know

Words in the Family

From Allen and Landaker (2005)

Tools for Teaching Academic Vocabulary by Janet Allen. Copyright © 2014. Stenhouse Publishers. All rights reserved.

Beyond Definitions

Concept, Term, Word, or Phrase	Usual Context (Often/Always)	Unusual Context (Rarely/Never)

Belongs to this family of words . . .	I would probably use this word if/when . . .

Tools for Teaching Academic Vocabulary by Janet Allen. Copyright © 2014. Stenhouse Publishers. All rights reserved.

"Defining" a Word

Reason why this word was used

_____

_____

_____

Target Word in Context

means . . .

How the word was used in the text we are reading

_____

_____

_____

_____

Antonyms are . . . .

Synonyms are . . . .

Example of when or why you would use this word:

Tools for Teaching Academic Vocabulary by Janet Allen. Copyright © 2014. Stenhouse Publishers. All rights reserved.

"Defining" a Word: scathing

Reasons for this scathing bulletin . . .
(60–61)

_____
_____
_____

Target Word in Context
" . . . issued a scathing bulletin "
(p. 60)

Scathing

_____ means . . .

Reason health officials in Angola resented the bulletin . . .

Example of why you would write a scathing letter/e-mail . . .

Synonyms for scathing are . . .

Antonyms for scathing are . . .

Tools for Teaching Academic Vocabulary by Janet Allen. Copyright © 2014 Stenhouse Publishers. All rights reserved.

Word Associations

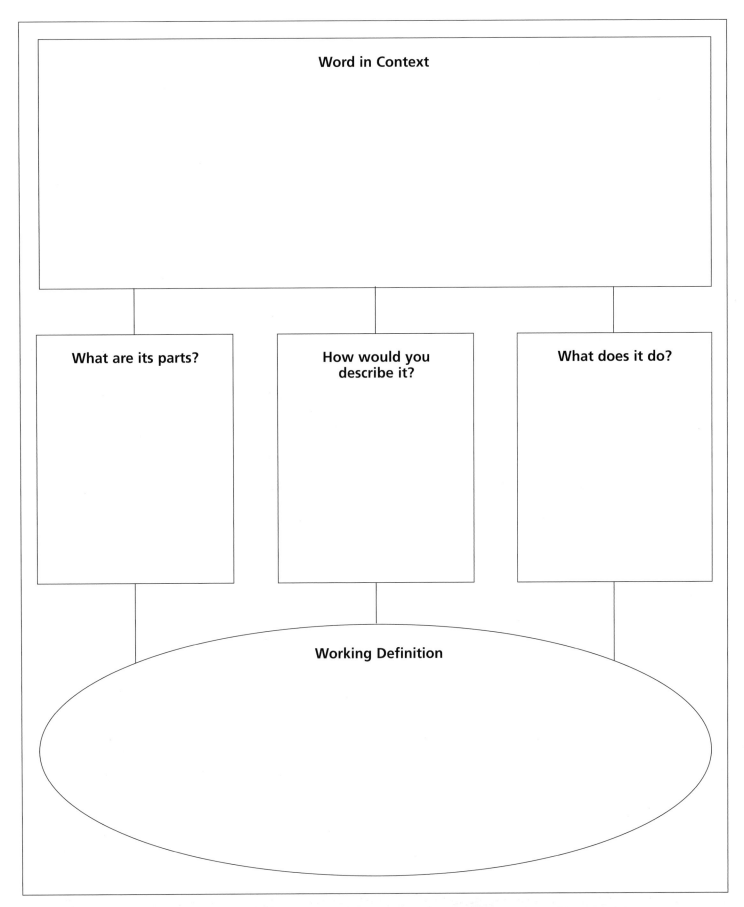

Word in Context

What are its parts?

How would you describe it?

What does it do?

Working Definition

Tools for Teaching Academic Vocabulary by Janet Allen. Copyright © 2014. Stenhouse Publishers. All rights reserved.

Word Associations: *bareback*

Word in Context

"The rules for <u>bareback</u> and saddle-bronc riding are short and tough:" (p. 17)

What are its parts?

bare (without covering or clothing)

back (rear part of body from neck to bottom of spine)

How would you describe it?

In a rodeo, bareback means the rider rides without a saddle.

What does it do?

Bareback describes a type of rodeo event.

Working Definition

The rider has to fight for balance on the horse's bare back: no saddle and only a rope to hang on to with one hand.

Tools for Teaching Academic Vocabulary by Janet Allen. Copyright © 2014. Stenhouse Publishers. All rights reserved.

Planning for Strategy Instruction

Introduction/Anticipation

- Find the "hook" for the concept.
- Specify/define what students will learn.
- Identify language that needs to be taught.

Modeled Lesson

- What resource(s) will you use?
- How will you "think aloud" the process or steps for this strategy?

Guided Learning/Independent Practice

- Ask students to note the attributes of the strategy.
- Choose a resource where students can practice the modeled lesson.
- Create a graphic/guide to support learning.

Closure

- Revisit steps in strategy.
- Students chart or record steps in the strategy in academic journals.
- Plan for transfer to other text type (more challenging, different genre).

Tools for Teaching Academic Vocabulary by Janet Allen. Copyright © 2014. Stenhouse Publishers. All rights reserved.

Word Knowledge LADDER

Target Word in Context

L

A

D

D

E

R

Tools for Teaching Academic Vocabulary by Janet Allen. Copyright © 2014. Stenhouse Publishers. All rights reserved.

Morpheme Math!

Morphemes are the smallest unit of meaningful language. A morpheme cannot be broken into smaller parts. If you know common morphemes used in math, it can help you figure out the meanings of lots of math terms.

bi- (two)	centi- (hundred)	circum- (around)	hexa- (six)
binomial	centimeter	circumference	hexagon

Using Prefixes to Learn New Words

Directions: Check your prefix list and note the common definitions of these prefixes. Use your knowledge of prefixes to predict what the words using these prefixes mean. Then, find two other words using each prefix where the prefix fits the definition on your list.

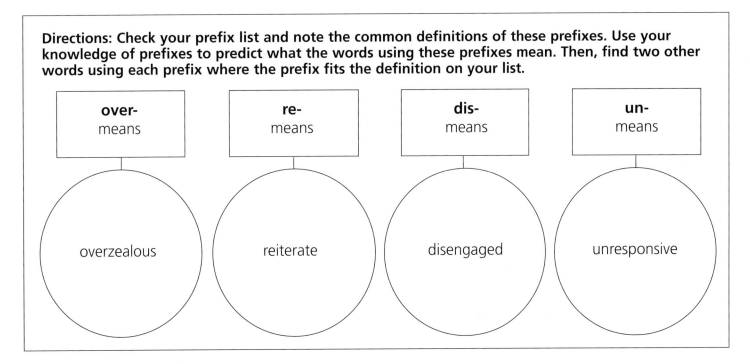

over- means	**re-** means	**dis-** means	**un-** means
overzealous	reiterate	disengaged	unresponsive

Tools for Teaching Academic Vocabulary by Janet Allen. Copyright © 2014. Stenhouse Publishers. All rights reserved.

Using Word Parts to Learn New Words

Directions: Discuss the word part in each of the boxes below and note possible meanings for each word part. Then, list three or more words that use this word part in a way that matches the definition(s) you noted.

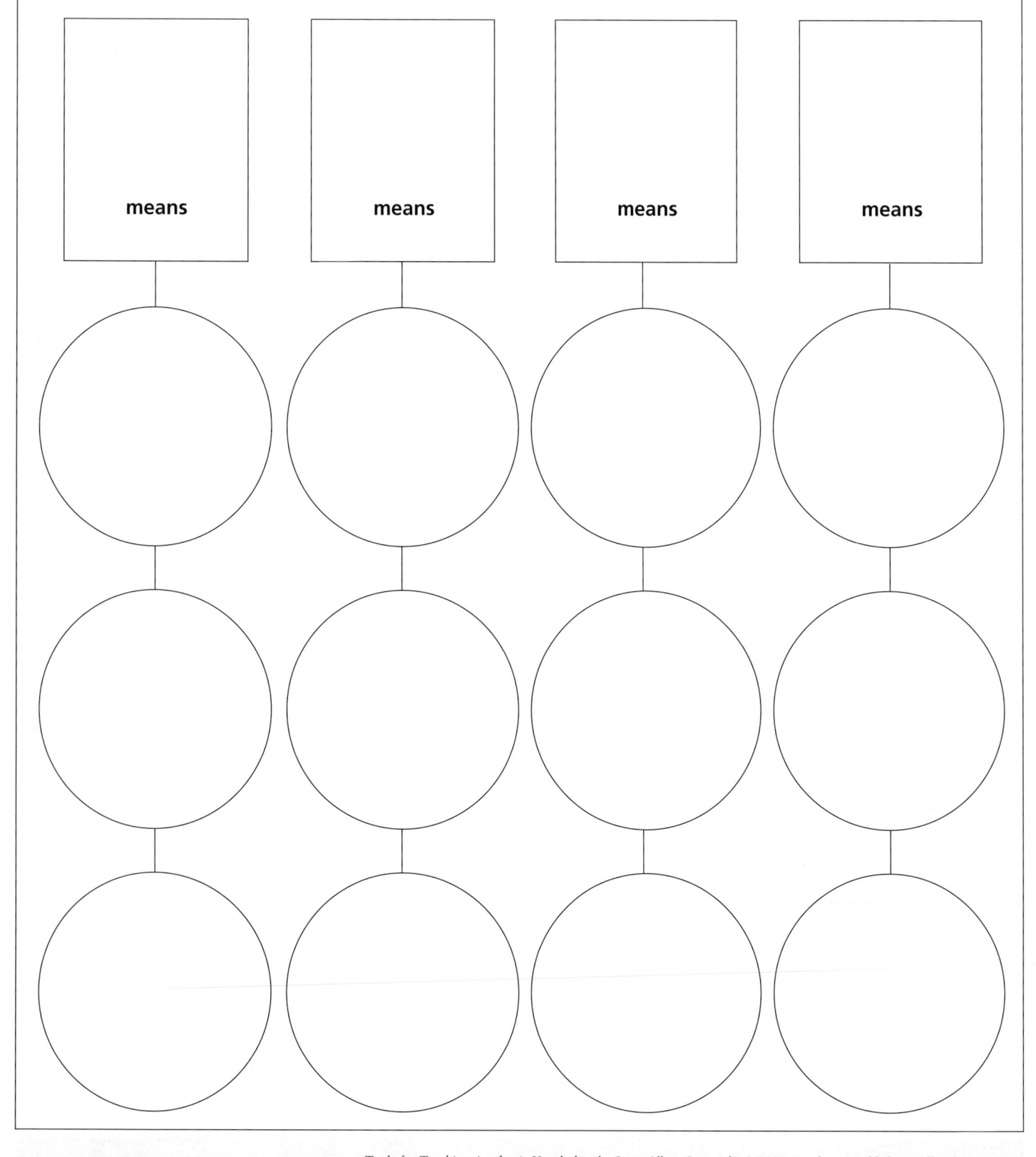

means

means

means

means

Tools for Teaching Academic Vocabulary by Janet Allen. Copyright © 2014. Stenhouse Publishers. All rights reserved.

Using Structural Analysis to Predict Meaning

Word Parts I've Learned:

Affixed Word	Word Parts	Meaning of Elements

Structural analysis means . . .

When we use structural analysis to figure out unknown words, we use these word parts in the following ways:

prefix:

root or base word:

suffix:

Tools for Teaching Academic Vocabulary by Janet Allen. Copyright © 2014. Stenhouse Publishers. All rights reserved.

Using Structural Analysis to Predict Meaning

Structural analysis means . . . .

breaking a word down into meaningful elements in order to predict what the word means based on knowing the meaning of each element.

Word Parts I've Learned:

Affixed Word	Word Parts	Meaning of Elements
paganism (8)	pagan + ism	–ism means practice or custom
scapulimancy (19)		
mythology (28)		

When we use structural analysis to figure out unknown words, we use these word parts in the following ways:

prefix: A word part at the beginning of a word. It creates a new word.

root or base word: Provides most of a word's meaning; usually from Greek or Latin.

suffix: Added at the end of the root word and can note something about a word's use or state.

Tools for Teaching Academic Vocabulary by Janet Allen. Copyright © 2014, Stenhouse Publishers. All rights reserved.

Troy Cunningham's Visual Puzzle

Tools for Teaching Academic Vocabulary by Janet Allen. Copyright © 2014. Stenhouse Publishers. All rights reserved.

Get a Clue!

Type of Context Clue	Description of Context Clue	Example
Definition		
Description		
Restatement		
Example		
Synonym or Antonym		
Compare or Contrast		
Apposition		
Visual (font, punctuation)		
Other		
Context clue notes:		

Tools for Teaching Academic Vocabulary by Janet Allen. Copyright © 2014. Stenhouse Publishers. All rights reserved.

Get a Clue!

Type of Context Clue	Description of Context Clue	Example
Definition	meaning provided in a direct statement	The word *amphibian* means "double life" or "two lives." (5)
Description	context provides description of characteristics, qualities of word	In front of these are pedipalps—clawed arms with pincers at the ends. (14)
Restatement	states again in a new way	Remember, the order of frogs is Anura—Greek for "no tail." (8)
Example	context provides an example representing word's meaning	There were growing reports of frogs that were deformed—for example, missing a rear leg. (28)
Synonym or Antonym	meaning expressed in terms that are similar or dissimilar	Glands in their skin produce poisons (toxins) that can make a predator sick or even kill it. (18)
Compare or Contrast	meaning expressed in words that are like or not like the word	This book is about real, not imaginary, scorpions. (7)
Apposition	uses parenthetical word or phrase to clarify/define	If necessary, however, it can stay on hot sand by "stilting"—standing tall on its legs, keeping the body away from the surface. (17)
Visual (font, punctuation)	uses visual to cue the reader to meaning of the word	Another threat is the chytrid (kit-rid) fungus, which has killed frogs in all sorts of habitats. (30)
Other		

Context clue notes:

Tools for Teaching Academic Vocabulary by Janet Allen. Copyright © 2014. Stenhouse Publishers. All rights reserved.

Finding the Clues

Sentence	Helpful Clues

Challenges when using context clues:

If context clues don't help, what else could you do?

Tools for Teaching Academic Vocabulary by Janet Allen. Copyright © 2014 Stenhouse Publishers. All rights reserved.

Expanding Definitions

Background Knowledge: Discuss the following words and make a prediction about what you think these words mean based on your background knowledge.

Context Clues: Read the following passage where the words above appear. Discuss the words in context and add information about each word's meaning based on the new information you gain from the context.

Dictionary: Now use a print or online dictionary to add new information to each word's meaning.

1.

2.

3.

4.

5.

6.

7.

8.

9.

Tools for Teaching Academic Vocabulary by Janet Allen. Copyright © 2014. Stenhouse Publishers. All rights reserved.

Identifying Text Features: Dictionary

Text Feature	Definition/Purpose	Example
• **Guide words**	Guide words are words printed at the top of a page of a dictionary indicating first and last entry word on that page.	
• **Entry word**	This is word you are searching, bold-faced, alphabetized.	
• **Pronunciation key**	Appears after the entry word; set apart with ( ); online symbol for hearing the word and ? shows punctuation key.	
• **Part of speech**	Shows how the word is used grammatically; part of speech shown with abbreviation.	
• **Definition**	Provides meaning of the word beginning with most common definition followed by other definitions in numbered order.	
• **Alternate spelling**	Also called variant spelling; follows entry; set apart with "also"; alternate spellings are boldface.	
• **Origin (derivation)**	Indicates time and languages of first-known use. Shows how meaning has changed from original to current use.	
• **Example sentences**	Show entry being used in a variety of sentences; *indicates audio to hear a sentence.	
• **Related forms**	Show affixed and compound words for each new form of the word; part of speech for new form is indicated.	
• **Synonyms**	Show words that are nearly the same used in example sentences or phrases. Sometimes show shades of meaning.	
• **Audio**	Online dictionaries have symbol indicating sound available for pronunciation and example sentence.	
• **Usage notes**	Show variety of ways word can be used. Online dictionaries show entry as used in other dictionaries (medical, science, math, cultural, etc.)	
•		

Tools for Teaching Academic Vocabulary by Janet Allen. Copyright © 2014. Stenhouse Publishers. All rights reserved.

If the Dictionary Could Talk

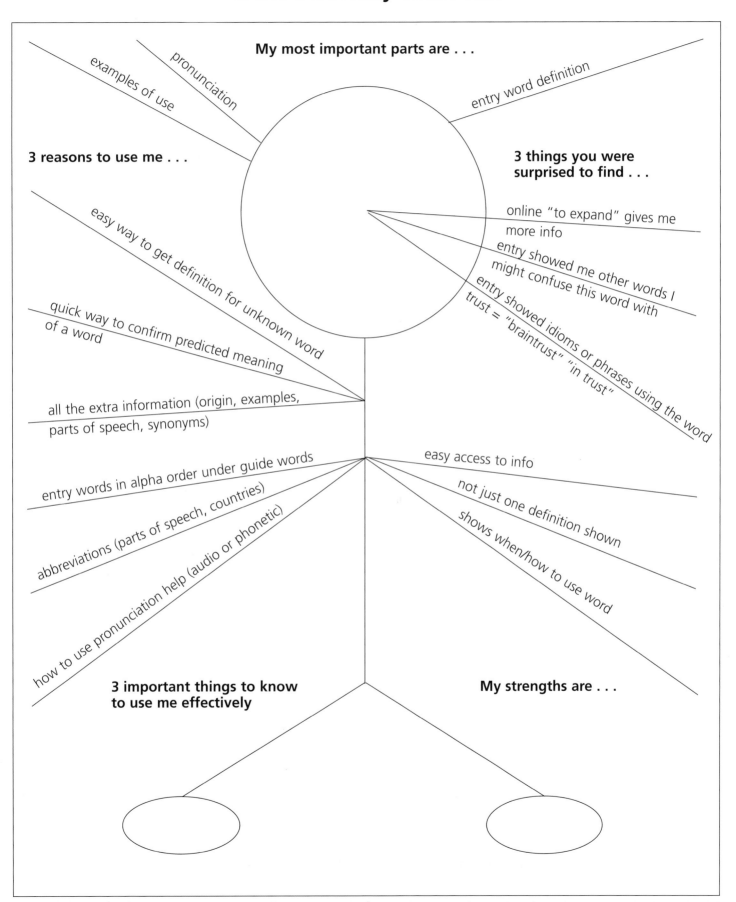

My most important parts are . . .

examples of use

pronunciation

entry word definition

3 reasons to use me . . .

3 things you were surprised to find . . .

easy way to get definition for unknown word

quick way to confirm predicted meaning of a word

all the extra information (origin, examples, parts of speech, synonyms)

entry words in alpha order under guide words

abbreviations (parts of speech, countries)

how to use pronunciation help (audio or phonetic)

online "to expand" gives me more info

entry showed me other words I might confuse this word with

entry showed idioms or phrases using the word

trust = "braintrust" "in trust"

easy access to info

not just one definition shown

shows when/how to use word

3 important things to know to use me effectively

My strengths are . . .

Tools for Teaching Academic Vocabulary by Janet Allen. Copyright © 2014. Stenhouse Publishers. All rights reserved.

Identifying Text Features: Dictionary

Text Feature	Definition/Purpose	Example
• Guide words		
• Entry word		
• Pronunciation key		
• Part of speech		
• Definition		
• Alternate spelling		
• Origin (derivation)		
• Example sentences		
• Related forms		
• Synonyms		
• Audio		
• Usage notes		
•		

Tools for Teaching Academic Vocabulary by Janet Allen. Copyright © 2014. Stenhouse Publishers. All rights reserved.

If the Dictionary Could Talk

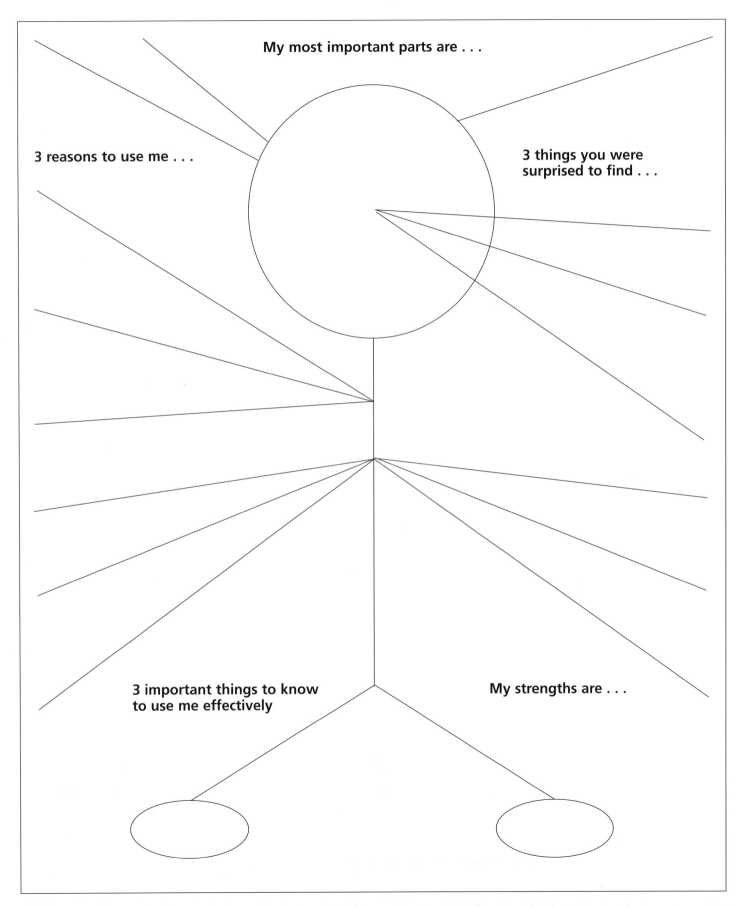

My most important parts are . . .

3 reasons to use me . . .

3 things you were surprised to find . . .

3 important things to know to use me effectively

My strengths are . . .

Tools for Teaching Academic Vocabulary by Janet Allen. Copyright © 2014. Stenhouse Publishers. All rights reserved.

Using the Right Word

Discuss each character from the text and decide which characters exhibit the characteristics shown in the matrix. If you don't know what the word means, use the context or other resources to determine meaning. If the word could describe the character, put a + in the space provided; put a – if the word would not describe the character. Put a ? in the space if you are undecided.

Descriptive Language	Reesa	Warren McMahon	Elizabeth McMahon	Luther Cully	Marvin Cully	Armetta Cully	"Doto"	Emmett Casselton	Harry T. Moore	J. D. Bowman
arrogant										
circumspect										
uppity										
fragile										
evil										
diligent										
patient										
inventive										
bold										
curt										
racist										
sedate										
melancholy										

Using the Right Word

Discuss each character from the text and decide which characters exhibit the characteristics shown in the matrix. If you don't know what the word means, use the context or other resources to determine meaning. If the word could describe the character, put a + in the space provided; put a – if the word would not describe the character. Put a ? in the space if you are undecided.

Descriptive Language										

Tools for Teaching Academic Vocabulary by Janet Allen. Copyright © 2014. Stenhouse Publishers. All rights reserved.

Tools for Teaching Academic Vocabulary by Janet Allen. Copyright © 2014. Stenhouse Publishers. All rights reserved.

Whose Talk? Understanding Language Register

Street Talk or Slang	Definition	Standard English	Context for Use

Tools for Teaching Academic Vocabulary by Janet Allen. Copyright © 2014. Stenhouse Publishers. All rights reserved.

A Pod of Dolphins?

Directions: Who knew there were so many ways to say *group*? Collective nouns are nouns that name a group of people, animals, or things. See if you can find the collective nouns that fit the groups of animals listed below.

1. A group of gorillas is called a ___*band*___.

2. A group of lions is called a ___*pride, sault, troop.*___.

3. A group of dogs can be called a ___*pack*___ or a ___*kennel*___ but if it is a group of puppies, it is called a ___*litter*___.

4. A group of monkeys is called a ___*tribe*___ or a ___*troop*___ of monkeys unless you are talking about chimpanzees. Then, the name changes to a _____ ___*cartload*___ of chimpanzees.

5. Cats, cats everywhere . . . but what do we call them? It depends on whether they are cats or kittens—whether they are wild or not.

   A group of house cats could be a ___*dout*___ or a ___*nuisance*___.

   A group of kittens would be a ___*kindle (kendle)*___ or a ___*litter*___.

   But a group of wild cats would be called a ___*destruction*___.

6. When you go swimming, you probably wouldn't want to be surprised by one shark so you certainly don't want to see a group of sharks! If you did see a group of sharks, that group would be called a ___*school*___ of sharks or a ___*shiver*___ of sharks.

Now it is your turn. See if your group can stump the other groups by creating a collective noun game. Use language books as well as Internet resources to find some interesting collective nouns that name groups of people, animals, or things.

1. Create your list of collective nouns. Be sure to keep an answer key!

2. Create some kind of game (puzzle, board, digital) for other students to text their knowledge of collective nouns.

3. Share your game with other groups. What new words did you learn?

Tools for Teaching Academic Vocabulary by Janet Allen. Copyright © 2014. Stenhouse Publishers. All rights reserved.

A Pod of Dolphins?

Directions: Who knew there were so many ways to say *group*? Collective nouns are nouns that name a group of people, animals, or things. See if you can find the collective nouns that fit the groups of animals listed below.

1. A group of gorillas is called a _____.

2. A group of lions is called a _____.

3. A group of dogs can be called a _____ or a _____ but if it is

   a group of puppies, it is called a _____.

4. A group of monkeys is called a _____ or a _____

   of monkeys unless you are talking about chimpanzees. Then, the name changes to a _____

   _____ of chimpanzees.

5. Cats, cats everywhere . . . but what do we call them? It depends on whether they are cats or

   kittens—whether they are wild or not.

   A group of house cats could be a _____ or a _____.

   A group of kittens would be a _____ or a _____.

   But a group of wild cats would be called a _____.

6. When you go swimming, you probably wouldn't want to be surprised by one shark so you

   certainly don't want to see a group of sharks! If you did see a group of sharks, that group

   would be called a _____ of sharks or a _____

   of sharks.

Now it is your turn. See if your group can stump the other groups by creating a collective noun

game. Use language books as well as Internet resources to find some interesting collective nouns

that name groups of people, animals, or things.

1. Create your list of collective nouns. Be sure to keep an answer key!

2. Create some kind of game (puzzle, board, digital) for other students to text their knowledge of

   collective nouns.

3. Share your game with other groups. What new words did you learn?

Tools for Teaching Academic Vocabulary by Janet Allen. Copyright © 2014. Stenhouse Publishers. All rights reserved.